herb gardening from the ground up

herb gardening
from the ground up

Everything you need to know
about growing your favorite herbs

Sal Gilbertie and Larry Sheehan

ILLUSTRATIONS BY LAUREN JARRETT

TEN SPEED PRESS
Berkeley

This is a revised edition, with new illustrations, of a work originally published in
the United States as *Herb Gardening at Its Best* by Atheneum Publishers in 1978.
Published in the United States by Ten Speed Press, an imprint of the Crown
Publishing Group, a division of Random House, Inc., New York.
www.crownpublishing.com
www.tenspeed.com

Ten Speed Press and the Ten Speed Press colophon are registered trademarks
of Random House, Inc.

Library of Congress Cataloging-in-Publication Data
Gilbertie, Sal.
    Herb gardening from the ground up : everything you need to know about
growing your favorite herbs / Sal Gilbertie and Larry Sheehan. — 1st ed.
        p. cm.
    Includes index.
1. Herb gardening. 2. Herb gardens. I. Sheehan, Larry. II. Title. III. Title:
Everything you need to know about growing your favorite herbs.
    SB351.H5G545 2012
    635'.7—dc23

                                        2011027436

ISBN 978-1-60774-029-2 (alk. paper)
eISBN 978-1-60774-080-3

Printed in the United States of America

Cover and interior design by Katy Brown
Cover photographs © Rachel Weill/Media Bakery (right)
and Ron Levine/Media Bakery (left)

10 9 8 7 6 5 4 3 2 1

First Ten Speed Press Edition

For Giovanni de Bernardone, who taught me
to thank God every day for the
wondrous gift of herbs.

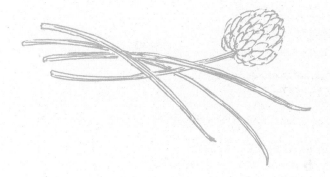

CONTENTS

III. HERB GARDEN PLANS [95]

IV. HERB CULTURE GUIDE [183]

I.

Herbs Are for Everyone

IN HIS MOST FAMOUS PRAYER, *Canticle of the Creatures*, St. Francis of Assisi praises God for all creation, including "Sister Earth, who produces all sorts of fruit and colored flowers and herbs." I had always been exposed to flowers, fruits, and vegetables because of our family business, but herbs came into my life quite by chance, and what a great blessing that chance encounter has proved to be! Not a day goes by without my learning something new and exciting about these fascinating and wondrous plants. I just can't wait to get up every morning and begin another day in my world of herbs, whether I am planting, lecturing, cooking, selling, or just breathing in the fragrances of herbs in our greenhouses and gardens.

I can't say no to any invitation to talk about herbs. On hundreds of occasions I have spoken to all kinds of groups—gardeners, farmers, cooks, teachers, children, oldsters—and I love it when I am asked questions about herbs at the end of these talks. What's another hour when you love what you're talking about and having fun, too?

My discovery of herbs and their multiple purposes and joys has been one of the most important things in my life. Through herbs I've strengthened my faith, enriched my family bonds, built a career that's rewarding to me on many levels, and struck up friendships with a host of fellow herb enthusiasts across the country. My passion for herbs has a lot to do with what I have found to be their essential, everlasting goodness. In these small, unassuming plants are found qualities and properties that can only be accounted for by some profound providential intelligence.

Thank God for herbs.

Herbs are so easy to grow, and so universal in their appeal and utility, that I believe there is room for an herb garden in everyone's life. That's the spirit in which this book has been conceived. Our approach to herb gardening is based on a broad understanding of the cultivation and care of herbal plants in a wide variety of landscapes great and small. It is designed to permit gardeners, from novices to experts, to enjoy herbs according to their own tastes and needs, and the particular time and space available to them.

The secret to success in growing herbs lies in the techniques of plant culture we at Gilbertie's Herb Gardens have developed over four generations in the business. Today, we grow nearly 500 varieties of herbs, including subspecies, and although culinary herbs account for 85 percent of our volume, about one-third of our customers also purchase and grow herbs for use beyond the kitchen. As one of the largest wholesale growers of potted herb plants in the country, we have a "big picture" of the ever-growing, ever-changing consumer demand for herbs. At the same time, through our busy retail garden center in Westport, Connecticut, we have come to know the down-to-earth wants and needs of home gardeners of every stripe.

Dispensing advice on growing and maintaining plants of any kind is akin to a fine art, and over the years we have learned the value of clarity and precision in giving instructions. This book sets out to achieve the same objectives for our readers as we've achieved in our gardener-to-gardener conversations with our customers.

Our first step will be to describe the optimum location and soil conditions for the basic herb garden. Then we will offer detailed profiles of the fifteen most popular culinary herbs, emphasizing the nuts-and-bolts methods for sowing and growing them most effectively. By becoming familiar with each of the basic herbs, you will learn the growing techniques that work for virtually all herbs.

In other words, once we have helped you figure out how to successfully grow parsley, which is a biennial, for use in your salads and sauces and as a garnish, then you automatically know how to grow caraway, also a biennial, for your rye-bread-baking projects, or watercress, for its tangy bite in sandwiches, salads, and soups. If you understand how to propagate and care for sage or rosemary, then you can use the same techniques on lavender, a similar single-stemmed perennial. Annual herbs, such as basil, coriander, and dill—

plants that, for all practical purposes, live for only the duration of a single season—also call for growing methods special to this category.

Once we have our cultural information in place, we will offer plans for dozens of herb gardens of broad interest, so as to acquaint you with the wide range of growth patterns among herbs, as well as their nearly infinite variety of leaf shapes and flower colors, and possibly inspire you to venture beyond the confines of the basic kitchen herb garden. The majority of these plans will be presented in an 8' x 8' planting scheme, to provide a common standard that all readers can consult in developing gardens for their own special sites.

There is no rule stating that herb gardens must be laid out in formal patterns, so as long as the right cultural conditions are present, the plants themselves will not suffer, even if the garden looks as if it were designed by a gardener wearing a blindfold. Generally, formal gardens laid out in geometric forms require more care than the rough-and-ready garden plot. But don't automatically reject the idea of a formal garden plan or associate it with pretense and privilege. The fact is, gardens organized with semicircular beds and crisscrossing pathways create as much perimeter as possible, not only for aesthetic effect but also to enable the gardener to tend and harvest herbs more conveniently.

The possibilities for theme gardens using herbs are endless, because in many categories, such as thyme or mint, there are multiple varieties and subspecies. Herbs may be grouped in families to bring pleasure and satisfaction to gardeners who have the same zeal for collecting as folks enamored of rare coins or stamps. We also offer garden plans for gardeners faced with asymmetrical spaces and unconventional growing conditions. Herbs can be used to cope with problem borders or semi-shady locations. Acknowledging the increasing popularity of container gardening, we also show how herbs can be adapted successfully for window boxes, whiskey barrels, troughs, and other planting vessels.

I believe it is the universality of herbs that makes me think no one should be without a garden containing a selection of these wonderful plants. And if you need more incentive, note that it is easier to be more successful, more quickly, with herbs than it is with flowers or vegetables, not to mention some of the more exotic houseplants. Herbs don't require as much space, as rich a soil, or as much attention after they are planted as flowers and vegetables do.

Certainly there are herbs to suit everyone's taste and lifestyle. If you're a party-giver, you can grow lemon verbena for martinis, mints for iced teas, and sweet woodruff for May wine. If beekeeping is your passion, you may want to take home several flats of borage and thyme to plant for your bees and thus favorably influence the flavor of your honey. If you're a salad lover, you can devote your growing space to rows of tangy greens like arugula, salad burnet, and sorrel. If you can't sleep, you can brew a cup of chamomile tea, justly famous for its calming effects, and await the sweet dreams you so deserve. Herbs even contribute to the care of the elderly, for whom it has been found that the introduction of lavender, in fresh or dried form, has a palliative effect.

In the kitchen, herbs are used to flavor vinegars, jellies, meat and fish rubs, and salad dressings. Speaking of salads, my godmother, Antoinette, used to gather greens for us as she traveled from her home in New Jersey to ours in Connecticut. Along the roadside and in the fields, she would pick dandelion greens, plantain, purslane, cardoon, and other herbs that grow wild. What we thought of as weeds (although we didn't dare use that word in Antoinette's presence) in fact made piquant additions to our more conventional lettuce mixes. Since then I've always thought of my godmother as the Italian Euell Gibbons—he who became famous showing people how to gather edibles from a wild landscape.

You can grow herbs simply for the aesthetic value of their diverse foliage or the contrasting or complementary color schemes available, especially in grays and greens, as demonstrated in a number of our garden plans. If you are primarily a flower grower, you can plant herbs, such as hyssop, borage, and sage alongside your flowers, both for their uses in the kitchen and their attractive blooms. Fennel and dill plants have foliage of such elegance that the addition of their tall stems make beautiful flower bouquets look even better.

Nowadays, herb gardening is gender-neutral. In early America, the garden was the exclusive responsibility of the woman of the house. But today, just as men have taken on their share of kitchen tasks, including the preparation of meals, they have also joined their partners in the garden. Herbs are not for women only, nor for people in any particular age bracket. The so-called "slow food" movement, the rise of sustainable agriculture, and the values implicit in the support of an organic food supply all have brought more and more young people into the world of herbs.

Herbs really are for everyone, and for all occasions. The Christmas Eve supper that my wife, Marie, and I host every holiday season for the Gilbertie clan is a good example of an occasion in which herbs, with their intrinsic flavors and rich symbolic meanings, play an important role. The centerpiece of our formal holiday table is a wreath that I fashion from cedar, boxwood, and holly, combined with bay, rosemary, golden thyme, lamb's ear, and tricolor sage. To this basic arrangement I add fresh white roses, white daisies, and sprigs of eucalyptus. Four white taper candles spaced evenly in the wreath shed their light on the foliage in all its colors and patterns.

At the place settings for all our female guests, I set out a white or red rose along with three or four sprigs of herbs, usually thyme (for courage), sage (for longevity), rosemary (for remembrance), and parsley (for festivity). When we all sit down, I take a moment to remind everyone of the symbolic associations of those herbs—just in case they've forgotten my disquisition from the previous year.

The supper marking *la viglia di natale* is a fish-lover's feast in the Italian tradition, prepared to perfection by Marie and the other great cooks among our relatives. Seven varieties of fish are prepared according to recipes that have been in our families for generations. Herbs provide the dominant flavors throughout the menu. Sautéed shrimp, for example, is seasoned with fresh savory, oregano, and parsley. Our Christmas Eve spaghetti—to which we add chopped filberts, pine nuts, walnuts, anchovies, and raisins—is enhanced with minced thyme, oregano, and garlic. The baked calamari dish uses bruised lemon verbena leaves, minced dill, savory, and parsley, and more garlic than the average cook would consider. Broiled salmon is prepared with minced shallots in a lemony dill and fennel sauce.

No one is hungry at the Gilberties' by the end of Christmas Eve, nor is anyone untouched by the magic of herbs.

Herb Varieties, New and Improved

In response to the growing popularity of herbs, many new cultivated varieties have been developed over the past decade. You may want to try some of the following newly introduced varieties in your own garden and in your favorite recipes.

Basil • Aussie Sweetie

This excellent variety is sometimes referred to as a Greek columnar basil because it grows quite erect—as tall as 36" if not pruned. With its slender profile, it takes up very little space in the garden. Its dark green foliage has a desirably strong basil flavor. Unlike most basils, it performs quite well indoors during the winter months. It lends itself to training as a topiary standard and as such strikes an elegant profile in a sunny window location in the home. (Because it is a sterile plant, the Aussie Sweetie cannot be grown from seed but must be propagated from cuttings.)

Oregano • Hot and Spicy

This variation on Greek oregano, developed by a Dutch hybridizer, packs a fiery edge that will spice up any meal. It grows in a compact bush form and is a good choice for container planting. Its rich green leaves often grow on red stems, so sprigs of Hot and Spicy make a decorative and tasty garnish on pizzas.

Stevia

An herbal alternative to sugar, the leaves of this plant, which grows wild as a small shrub in Brazil and Paraguay, can be used fresh, dried, powdered, or extracted as a liquid to sweeten a variety of beverages and foods. It is grown from seed as an annual and for best results should be harvested just as its flowers appear. Stevia tolerates light shade but do not transplant into the garden until temperatures are above 50°F.

Rosemary • Barbecue

This is a dark green variety with a strong, erect growing habit and the same intense flavor of most rosemaries. It is especially welcome in poultry dishes of every kind. As a tender perennial, it must be brought indoors in the Northeast in October and November, where it will survive the winter in a cool, well-lit location. The stems of this variety make excellent skewers on the grill.

Sage • Berggarten

This variety, originating in Germany, grows as a compact bush with rounded, very large silver-gray leaves and lilac-blue flowers. Like most sages, it does best in hot and dry conditions, and even though it is touted as mildew-resistant, don't be tempted to wet its foliage with the sprinkler. It's an attractive plant in the garden with a strong sage flavor wonderful for cooking.

English Thyme • Wedgewood

A sport of common thyme, this herb has variegated foliage, chartreuse and dark green, and pale lavender flowers. Leaves have the aromatic thyme flavor desired by cooks. One of its best features is that it does not develop the woody stems that most English thymes have in their second and third years of growth.

Herbs: Yesterday, Today, and Tomorrow

"SAL, THERE'S NO MARKET FOR HERB PLANTS," my fellow growers used to tell me. "Just grow parsley and chives. That's all people ever ask for."

When I first started growing an expanded range of herbs commercially in 1959, they thought I was downright crazy. "Herbs are for witches and warlocks," one of them told me. He apparently thought I was planning to sell my herbs to help people ward off evil spirits, cure lunacy, reverse balding, and protect cows.

The shelf life of these thirteenth-century superstitions is pretty amazing; as recently as the 1950s, there was still resistance to herbs across the board. Except for chives and curly parsley—and the mint for mint juleps—most grocery stores and supermarkets did not even carry herbs in their produce departments. If a home cook wanted to incorporate fresh herbs into a recipe, he or she had to grow them in the home garden, and not many cooks did that, either.

People actually worried that the use of herbs would somehow ruin recipes. Salt was relied on heavily to impart flavor, or the illusion of flavor, to daily meals. Use of pepper ran a distant second in most kitchens. Then there were the numerous sodium-based blends, such as MSG, that allowed one to sprinkle on flavor with a shake of the wrist. Combine that with canned fruits and vegetables, frozen dinners, white bread, and Hostess cupcakes, and say farewell to Gourmet Nation.

Then, in her groundbreaking television show, "The French Chef," Julia Child dared to say the words *bouquet garni*. The phrase refers to a collection of herbs used to flavor soup, stocks, and stews. Typically a bay leaf is combined with sprigs of parsley and thyme; some recipes add other herbs as well, such as basil, chervil, and tarragon. Julia showed us with kindergarten simplicity how to tie up the herbs with a piece of string and then how to use them to prepare such dishes as *boeuf Bourguignon, blanquette de veau, osso buco*, and *bouillabaisse*. The dishes had suspicious-sounding foreign names, but Julia's easygoing manner, clear instructions, and warbling laughter made all the recipes sound doable and delicious.

With her long-running television program and speaking tours and through her many books, Julia Child legitimized the value of serious cooking and the central role of fresh herbs as a catalyst for flavor for untold numbers of previously kitchen-challenged Americans.

Other trailblazers followed in Julia's footsteps, most notably Martha Stewart. Her spectacular multimedia career—encompassing cooking, gardening, decorating, collecting, and just about anything else of interest and importance to the modern woman—got its start in Westport, Connecticut. She was a frequent visitor to Gilbertie's Garden Center in Westport in those days, gathering herb plants for her numerous garden projects and for her own gardens. After her own show was launched on television, she invited me to appear on a number of occasions to impart ideas and information for sowing and growing herbs, even as she demonstrated their versatility in flavoring food dishes of all kinds. Most recently, Martha and I worked together on the revamping of the herb garden at the New York Botanical Gardens in the Bronx. I supplied the herbs; Martha helped to update the original formal, English-style design from the 1950s. A perimeter planting of 1,000 of our herb plants encompassed the geometric pattern of dark green boxwood bushes, silver cardoon, and golden sage in the center.

Martha Stewart's culinary path reflects the shifts that have taken place in America's food culture over the past several decades, and in the important role of herbs in that culture. Food has gone from the frying pan to the pedestal. Chefs have gone from working stiffs to superstars. There are almost as many cookbooks published every year as murder mysteries. There are more cooking classes offered than English-as-a-second-language classes. Restaurants get trendier and trendier. It takes a PhD in gastronomy to understand some menus. The Food Network and other cable channels provide a non-stop, all-you-can-eat buffet of programs devoted to cooking and eating, and if you're still hungry, you can go online.

Now that herbs have entered the mainstream, herb plants and herbal products are widely available. Growers from around the world compete to satisfy the appetite for herbs. As I mentioned earlier, we grow more than 500 varieties of certified organic herb plants. These include numerous cultivars (especially in such prolific families as basil, mint, rosemary, sage, and thyme; rosemary alone comes in some ninety varieties, growing upright or prostrate, with different flower colors, leaf characteristics, and essential oil contents.) Although our primary market is culinary herbs, we have many customers who take home our plants for their fragrance, for their healing and healthful properties, and for use in teas and infusions, as dyes, and even as pest repellents.

The term *organic*, by the way, is especially meaningful when it is applied to culinary herbs. Herbs grown on a large scale with the help of liquid nitrogen fertilizers have more foliage, so if they are sold to supermarkets by the pound, they make more money for the grower. The problem is that the use of chemical fertilizers diminishes the oil content, reducing and sometimes altering flavor. Many of our astute customers have remarked on this difference, observing that store-bought basil and cilantro are weak in flavor compared to our certified organically grown plants and the herbs they grow in their gardens.

Because herbs take so little space to grow, virtually everyone is capable of raising his or her own intensely flavorful organic herbs for use in the kitchen or in their many other applications. Even if you do not have access to a sunny location in a yard, containers, such as window boxes or patio planters make it possible to gain control of this small but important part of your food supply, and by extension gain access in your cooking to what I like to call "flavor that does us a favor, flavor you can savor."

The Gilbertie family's venture into commercial farming took on many different shapes over the years. Like many American success stories, it all began on a boat sailing from Europe, bound for New York City. My grandfather, Antonio, was seventeen when he first came to the United States in the late 1880s. I can only imagine the sensations he experienced, coming from the small village of San Michele in the countryside northeast of Naples, Italy, to visit his uncle in bustling, boisterous Brooklyn. Family history is obscure on the subject, but somehow during this visit, Antonio discovered Westport, Connecticut, then a sparsely populated rural township on Long Island Sound. Legend has it that he fell in love with Compo Beach, a public beach that still attracts throngs of visitors every summer. It reminded him of the beaches around Naples, on the Tyrrhenian Sea.

Returning to Italy, Antonio married Maria Celeste and sired four children, but the dream of Compo Beach remained alive in him. Finally, in 1902, he made his move. He immigrated to America with his wife and children, as well as with three brothers—Michael, Samuel, and Julius—and a nephew, also named Michael. It was a loss to the population of San Michele but an injection of fresh blood for Westport.

The four adult male Gilberties all landed jobs at the Fillow Flower Company in Westport, which grew cut flowers in greenhouses covering sixty acres, shipping tens of thousands of stems daily by rail into the lucrative New York market. Carnations, roses, snapdragons, and pansies were the company's biggest sellers. It was also known for a long-stemmed flower it had hybridized, called the Fillow Pansy. No small operation, Fillow employed 300 employees, most of them Italians "fresh off the boat," as the expression went in those days.

Hard work enabled Antonio to accumulate a small nest egg over the years. In 1922, at the age of fifty-four, he decided to go into business for himself. He bought a four-acre lot on Sylvan Road in Westport, near the Norwalk line, for $4,000. He retained two acres, complete with house and barn, and sold the rest of the parcel to the adjoining Westport Country Club (now Birchwood Country Club) for $2,000, giving him some welcome capital to work with. He purchased several used greenhouses from other growers, moved them onto the property, and put up a sign: A. GILBERTIE, FLORIST.

Without the size or scale of the Fillow operation, Antonio carved out his own niche markets for flowers and soon had a viable business. He specialized in some of the flower varieties less common in that era—such as anemones, freesia, Gerber daisies, and ranunculus—shipping them into the city in bunches of twenty-five in much smaller quantities than Fillow traded in, and was therefore more likely to sell out.

Antonio hit the jackpot when he learned from a Dutch purveyor about a method for growing flowers from so-called pre-cooled bulbs. It enabled him to grow spring daffodils, irises, and tulips in his greenhouses at a faster rate. He became one of the first growers to ship cut flowers of spring bulb varieties into New York in time for the Christmas holidays and all through January and February. Like the farmer who gets corn to market by the Fourth of July, Antonio enjoyed immediate and widespread acceptance of his early spring flowers.

From his years with Fillow, my grandfather had mastered growing plants under glass with a circulating hot-water heating system. In his greenhouse range, the houses farthest from the heat source were always colder. He overcame that disadvantage by growing flowers that tolerated cooler temperatures, such as calendula and dianthus, along with many bulb flowers. He understood that in a small growing operation, maximum production per square foot was paramount.

When the Great Depression hit in 1929, vast portions of the economy were affected, but oddly enough, many cut-flower growers continued to thrive, or at least kept their heads above water. Flowers remained affordable expenses, apparently because fresh bouquets brought good cheer and a sense of hope to people. But not all growers survived. In 1933, a small greenhouse operation located on Isaac Street in the city of Norwalk, Westport's neighbor on its western border, went bankrupt. The bank holding the mortgage, which was itself sorely pressed financially, offered Antonio control of Norwalk Greenhouses for a year: no charge, no strings attached. If he could make it profitable at the end of that period, the business was his. By all accounts a demanding but fair employer and a shrewd businessman, Antonio succeeded. By year's end, he bought all the greenhouses, the business, and the property itself for $10,000.

As his business expanded, Antonio made more hires, mostly from within his own family. During this time, my father, Salvatore (Sal Senior), had been working as a reporter for the *Bridgeport Times-Star* (now the *Connecticut Post*) in nearby Bridgeport, home of P. T. Barnum of circus and freak show fame. Two of my father's brothers, Ed and Tony, worked for the same paper as linotype operators. (My father and Ed were born in the United States following the family's emigration.) When all three men were laid off at the same time, Antonio offered them jobs with A. GILBERTIE, FLORIST. Already in his employ was another son, John, trained as a plumber and responsible for the coal-fired hot-water heating system that served all the greenhouses, and his two sons-in-law, Angelo (married to Margaret) and Anthony (married to Frances).

Antonio sent Ed and Tony to run the Norwalk Greenhouses operation, and had Sal Senior work side by side with him in Westport. With a good head for business and the ability to learn all the intricacies of growing and caring for plants on the job, my father was given more and more responsibility. By the late 1930s, he had taken over the business from Antonio, who had fallen ill with heart disease (his wife had died years before).

Although he was confined to a wheelchair, the aging patriarch still wanted to stay active in the business in some way. Family members prodded my father to find something for his father to do—and my father, though well-intentioned, came up with a bad idea. He suggested to his father that Antonio station himself under the grape arbor he himself had planted, with one empty bucket and one bucket full of stones. Every time a customer arrived, he was to transfer a stone from one bucket to the other, as a way of obtaining an exact count of the daily customer flow. Antonio was so appalled by this proposition, which he considered demeaning, that he attempted to whack his son with his cane, a gesture he made with such force that he fell out of his wheelchair.

My grandfather was clearly a piece of work. I am told he took great exception to my being named Salvatore, instead of Antonio, when I was born in 1937, and that for three months he refused to even look at me. In contrast, when my sister was given his wife's name, Marie Celeste, upon her birth, he was overjoyed and showered her with gifts. Such are the powerful ways of the old country.

By the time Antonio died in 1944, my father had made a significant departure in the company's product line. The Gilbertie family had always maintained large vegetable gardens for their personal use. But with the nation at war, Sal now offered his customers a wide range of vegetable seedlings, as well as flowers, to meet a broad new public demand. The U.S. government—led by First Lady Eleanor Roosevelt, who set aside space for growing produce on the grounds of the White House—encouraged Americans to plant "victory gardens" to reduce pressure on food supplies during World War II and to bolster the morale of citizens on the home front. "A garden will make your rations go further!" one wartime poster proclaimed. An estimated twenty million families planted gardens in their backyards, in empty lots, and even on city rooftops. Women's magazines offered tips on growing and preserving garden produce. People began canning their vegetables and fruits with a vengeance. (The year 1943 saw sales of 315,000 pressure cookers, used in the canning process, compared to 66,000 in 1942.)

Victory gardens, or war gardens as some called them, were immense in size compared with the average family plot of today, and my father grew vegetable seedlings in sufficient quantities to fill them. The garden center's standard 12" x 24" flat held 108 seedlings of the same species. (As a boy, I always admired my muscular father's ability to carry two of those weighty flats, one cradled in each arm, to a customer's car.) The most popular vegetables were tomatoes, eggplant, peppers, squash, cucumbers, broccoli, cabbage, cauliflower, brussels sprouts, and lettuces. He also grew more specialized vegetables, such as kale, kohlrabi, endive, escarole, fennel, celery, and celeriac.

The demand for vegetable plants helped the business thrive during the war years. But my father faced a new challenge when the war ended: air freight. With the postwar growth of commercial aviation, the cut-flower growers in the tri-state area suddenly had serious competition from farmers in Florida, who flew fresh flowers into New York City in greater volume and at lower cost than Gilbertie's or other northern-climate wholesale growers could match.

My father decided to use his greenhouses to cultivate bulbs and potted plants that would have seasonal appeal. He grew red tulips for Valentine's Day; crocuses, daffodils, and hyacinths for early spring shows of color;

azaleas, calceolaria, and cineraria for Mother's Day; hydrangea and lilies for Easter; chrysanthemums and kalanchoe for Thanksgiving; and poinsettias, cyclamen, and Christmas cactus for Christmas.

Another customer base was provided by wealthy estates in Fairfield County. Head gardeners might have access to one small greenhouse on their own grounds to grow gardenias, orchids, and bulb flowers over the winter, but they needed help from commercial growers to maintain their landscapes and plant up their formal gardens, urns, and other ornate containers. Every fall we would receive large bedding plant orders for delivery the following spring—2,000 White Magic Petunias in 4" pots, for example, or 400 Enchantress Pink Geraniums. Nowadays there are garden centers and box stores with plenty of bedding plants to choose from in the spring, but at that time greenhouse operators were the sole supplier. Such orders kept our greenhouses full and our employees busy during the slow winter months.

In the fall of 1957, my father received a large order, not for flowering plants but for sixty plants of each of twelve different varieties of herbs commonly used in cooking, for delivery in May of 1958. That delivery date happened to coincide with my graduation from Fairfield University, when I joined my father's business full time.

The person who had ordered the herb plants was known around town as "the Baroness," a remote personality with aristocratic tastes and the wealth to indulge them. She had a greenhouse built for sunbathing on cool days. She had phones rigged up on trees throughout her estate so she could communicate with her workers without meeting them face to face.

One of her gardeners worked for the Baroness for three years without seeing her. He lost his job one day when she rang him up at some tree to order 300 rose bushes for a new garden area. He observed that he would also have to buy five or six cubic yards of cow manure to fertilize the new roses. She replied, "No one uses the word *manure* on the phone to me," and canned him on the spot.

The Baroness was a good customer. She ordered cut flowers by the pail, not the bunch, and if she liked a certain color in the roses, she'd buy six dozen twice a week. We would come to an anteroom of her mansion to make our deliveries. We'd ring the bell, announce ourselves through a speaker system, and wait for the buzzer to unlock the door. Then we'd come in with our flowers, set them on the floor in the empty room, and retreat outside. Then we'd wait for a few minutes until the buzzer sounded again. Then we'd go back inside and collect our payment, left where the flowers had been (we never saw the person who did the replacing), along with a small vial of White Shoulders, Golden Shadows, or The Baroness perfume. Our customer had made a fortune in the perfume business and always tipped us with a sample of her product.

Our herb plants were needed for a giant culinary herb garden the Baroness was planning to build, sixty feet in diameter, divided into twelve wedges of equal area, each area containing sixty herb plants. My father had never grown herb plants commercially—although he knew how to, having always included a number of them in our kitchen garden and mixed in with our perennial flowers and cutting garden. He used some herbs as companion plants to help keep pests away from certain vegetables—but mainly he grew them for our kitchen.

Still, my father did not want to disappoint the Baroness. That winter in the greenhouses, he planted not sixty but a hundred herbs in each of the twelve categories—to be sure he ended up with all he needed to fill her order. The plantings were particularly successful, so in the spring, when the herbs were ready for moving outdoors, he found himself with quite a surplus.

We delivered the big order to the Baroness, picked up our White Shoulders, and came back to the garden center. Then we put the extra herb seedlings, which had been moved into 4" pots, out with the rest of our plants. When they sold out—almost immediately—my father turned to me and said, "Sal, quick: learn about herbs."

Stalking the Elusive Pink Hyssop

MY EDUCATION IN HERBS began the day my father decided there might be a future in adding herb plants to our line of flowers, vegetables, and other plants. I soon discovered there were two main obstacles to my finding out about this remarkable family of plants, especially in terms of the specific knowledge that professional growers need to have.

First, there was a lack of clear-cut, detailed cultural information on herbs at that time. I obtained everything available on the subject from the U.S. Department of Agriculture, the Cooperative Extension Service at the University of Connecticut, and the local library, without finding much information on the practical aspects of growing herbs. Enough books have been written on these fascinating plants to fill a greenhouse, but most of the literature is devoted to lore and usage. It was easy to find out which herbs are related to which zodiac signs, or what Greeks used to think about sage, or how a tussy-mussy (a small herb bouquet) is constructed. But it was not easy to obtain accurate advice on how to grow the herbs. Only through trial and error, and frequent consultations with a group of friends I came to refer to as "the herb ladies," did I gradually develop the methods for sowing, growing, and maintaining herbs that I use today.

The second big problem I faced was that many sources for the herbs, and particularly for herbs started from seed, were unreliable. In those days the large seed companies, such as Burpee or Park, carried only the basic culinary herbs, so I had to deal with small herb farms and amateur herb growers to find a lot of the other herbs we needed.

I did not always get what we needed. It took me four years to locate a source for a seed that produced true dwarf basil—a small-leafed plant preferred for pots because of its compact growth. Seed dealers advertised dwarf basil, and I would order it, but because all types of basil seeds look alike, the only way to find out what we really had was to grow it to maturity.

It took seven years to locate hyssop seed that actually produced pink and white flowering hyssop instead of the common blue flowering kind, *Hyssop officinales*, which is not to be confused with anise hyssop, *Agastache foeniculum*, a perennial herb that is neither an anise nor a hyssop. The flowers don't emerge on hyssop until August, so each time I'd buy pink hyssop or white hyssop it took me almost an entire growing season from the time I sowed it in the spring to find out I had the blues.

To develop good herb seed really requires professional harvesting, storing, and packaging techniques—not to mention honesty in advertising one's wares. On one occasion I placed a substantial order for a wide range of seed through a mail-order firm that had sent me an impressive catalog. I enclosed my check for $63. A couple of weeks later I received a package with a fraction of the seed I had ordered and a refund check for $59. Many small seed catalogs made impressive offerings, I found, but often could not deliver on them.

A few years later, after I noticed sweet woodruff had become very popular, I ordered $10 worth of seed from a reputable company. It came in a package marked: "Germination Rate–92%." That told me I'd have all the sweet woodruff I could possibly use for the next season. But when I got around to growing it, I had problems. I used my normal sowing techniques, but nothing came up. I tried a propagation technique called stratification, which subjects the seed to conditions like the natural experience of overwintering (in this case, by freezing them), prompting them to sprout—but that didn't work either. I even tried cracking the shell and bathing it in sulfuric acid, but still nothing happened.

Finally I called up the company and said, "What's this about a 92 percent germination rate? I get 0 percent."

"But it's true," they responded. "When we cut open a sampling of the seeds, 92 percent were green and alive. However, we forgot to mention on the package that it takes a year from sowing for sweet woodruff to actually sprout."

Many seeds of herbs, I discovered, simply don't germinate unless they are sown soon after they are harvested. Sweet cicely and angelica are two that must be sown within two to three weeks after harvest or the seed fails to sprout in quantities worth the labor. I used to think bay seed just naturally had a low germination rate, but then I found that it too fared poorly "on the shelf." I would sow 7,000 bay seeds, acquired through a seed house in this country, and obtain less than 700 healthy plants. Then I began to get freshly harvested seed directly from Greece. When I sowed this seed, my germination rate for bay went from 10 to 80 percent.

Greek oregano was an herb I wanted to grow in quantity because it had a spicy kick that conventional oregano lacked. But I could not find a good source for the seed. One day, stopping by an Italian deli not far from our garden center in Westport, I discovered that Art, the proprietor, imported packages of dried Greek oregano with the seeds still at the top of the stem for his customers. He was selling them for 99 cents per package. I took a couple of packages back to the farm and began experimenting. By rolling the seed heads in the palms of my hands, I harvested the seed. Then I sowed it in flats for my own crop of Greek oregano. As it turned out, each batch of seeds produced seven distinctly different subspecies of the herb. The plants had been cross-pollinated by bees on the Greek islands where they grew in the wild. Some had tiny gray leaves on small, erect plants; others had large green leaves on larger, sprawling plants. But all seven varieties had the exact same flavor. If you chewed on a fresh leaf, it would always "bite" your tongue, and that's what I liked.

Growers and gardeners alike have been confused by the conflicting nomenclature sometimes used to identify herb plants, which in fact cover a wide range of botanical families. Keeping this theory of herbal relativity in mind, we can say that, basically, herbs are any soft-stemmed plants grown for their fragrance or flavor or for their value to well-being and beauty. They're not woody, like a shrub or tree is, and they're not exactly food crops, though some of them, such as onions, are as much food as flavor. And they're not spices, which come from the roots, bark, seeds, and fruits of tropical trees; think cardamom, cinnamon, ginger, nutmeg. Coriander is one of those rare plants that is both herb and spice. The feathery leaves of coriander, or cilantro, are the herb, and its seeds are the spice.

There's a kind of language barrier that has to be vaulted before people can appreciate herbs for what they are. It takes time and careful observation to differentiate between wild marjoram and sweet marjoram, say, or orange mint and peppermint, or French tarragon and its much-maligned imposter, Russian tarragon. And it takes forbearance to tolerate yet another pun on the word *thyme*, or to be told that the plant you're trying to buy is not dill but *Anethum graveolens*. Latin terms for plants are indispensable to advanced gardeners as a means of firmly identifying a plant from among dozens of similar varieties. But to the novice an excessive use of Latin smacks of snobbism.

I still have trouble with the terms used. One year we received an order for 1,000 plants for the famous herb gardens at the Cloisters in New York City. But all the plants were ordered by their true botanical names in Latin, and it took me half a day to translate them.

In any case, don't worry about what you call the different herbs. The word *herb* itself is rife with disputation. A friend of mine once gave a talk to a chapter of the Herb Society of America. Afterward she conducted a poll and discovered that even in those exalted circles there was divided opinion on how to pronounce the word. She found that half of the audience pronounced it "herb"—British-style with the h—and the other half followed the American example and said "erb" with the h silent. When I told a friend of mine about this linguistic divide, he remarked, "If they're going to call it 'erb garden, I say to 'ell with it."

So developing a dependable lineup of live herb plants was a challenge. And as I finally began to make some headway, I found that marketing the herbs was no easy matter, either.

There are legal obstacles to the dissemination of certain herbs. I can't ship tansy plants into some cattle-growing states, because it is outlawed. In those states it's regarded not as a useful herb, but as a threat to browsing livestock— if a pregnant cow eats any quantity, it induces a miscarriage. If you plant

St. John's wort in Connecticut, it grows at a normal pace and comes in handy for making infusions to treat anxiety. If you live in California, St. John's wort is a weed that spreads so fast it gives gardeners anxiety.

My own marketing missteps didn't always help the cause. Here's how they began. In 1969, when Simon and Garfunkel came out with their hit version of the traditional English folk song "Scarborough Fair," extolling the virtues of "parsley, sage, rosemary, and thyme," I decided it was time to launch our herb business on a big scale. Specifically, I had the brainstorm that I could sell a lot of herbs at the Great Danbury Fair, an annual event that took place about an hour's drive from our garden center. We rented a stall at the fairgrounds and spent ten days there trying to sell the 70,000 plants I had grown and potted for the occasion. Seven hundred thousand people walked by our booth during that period. We sold a total of 400 plants.

Obviously I was premature in my marketing plans—not to mention a bit naïve in expecting fairgoers to lug parsley around instead of cotton candy. In any case, times change. Less then ten years later, we opened a similar booth at a much smaller fair in New York and couldn't keep up with the business.

I attribute the growth in popularity of herbs since our Danbury Fair fiasco to the revival of interest in vegetable gardening and in good home cooking, and to the rise of the organic farming movement and its emphasis on self-reliance and the value of healthy foods and food habits. When low-salt and no-salt diets came into vogue as a means of coping with high blood pressure and other health issues, many more people turned to herbs to season their meals.

To reiterate an earlier and very important point, home-grown herbs are always better than store-bought herbs for cooking. Most commercial growers of culinary herbs use chemical fertilizers to stimulate leaf growth in the plants in order to get a bigger harvest. Generally, however, herbs that are forced into excessive growth are not as flavorful nor as healthful as those that grow at their normal rate in an organic soil bed.

Since the time of Hippocrates, herbs and spices have been valued for their curative effects. The herb garden at the National Library of Medicine in Washington, D.C., includes more than 100 herbs regarded as healing plants integral to the development of modern medicine.

I am no expert in herbal home remedies myself. But when I was a kid, my mother used to whip up a batch of rue and olive oil as a kind of balm for aching muscles. She'd brew chamomile tea for stomach aches. And if any of us ever looked a little peaked while we were growing up, she'd blame it on "worms" and make us eat a clove of garlic.

That's the extent of my direct experience of healing by herbs. But we still get enough customers buying horehound to make their own cough and cold remedies, or mugwort and valerian to sooth their digestive tracts, to know that the centuries-old practice of using herbs to promote health and well-being is still popular with a segment of the population. One important change I have noted in this area is the widespread availability of herbal products, not just in health food stores but also in many supermarkets.

Fashion is fickle in herbs as in anything else. One year customers can't get enough of lavenders and scented geraniums. The next, natural dye sources, such as bedstraw and yarrow are all the rage. More recently, thanks largely to an article in *Organic Gardening* on certain magical properties of comfrey, we sold all 2,000 of our pots of that herb in the month of May. Planning ahead, I was ready with 2,500 pots the next year. But that spring no one wrote anything about comfrey and I was stuck with the batch.

We folded some of the comfrey into our compost piles—the nitrogen-rich herb is a great compost-builder—tossed some of it into the chicken coop, and dumped the rest in a back lot. Now we have a field full of comfrey, which doesn't surprise me. I know by now that sometimes the less attention you give these herbs, the better they do. (Comfrey, by the way, is one of the few herbs that deer are attracted to. Otherwise, deer, which are so plentiful that they are pests in some areas, stay out of the herb garden.)

In detailing my education as a grower of herbs, I would be remiss not to thank "the herb ladies" who entered my life at an opportune time. They included a loyal customer from the early days. Mrs. Percy Cashmore, who lived in nearby Weston, Connecticut, happened to be president of the Herb Society of America at the time. She was a fount of helpful information on the varieties that she thought were the most important for me to cultivate. One day she handed me her copy of *Herbs: Their Culture and Uses* by Rosetta

Clarkson. Clarkson had died in 1950, long before my interest turned to herbs, but her knowledge and wit remain as fresh and relevant to gardeners as they were when Salt Meadows, her garden in Milford, Connecticut, was in its glory: "lifting us out of the hurrying present," as she wrote with her usual eloquence, "even for just a little while."

Anyway, her book was the answer to my prayers. It contained reliable and straightforward answers to all the questions I had about the propagation of herbs, whether by sowing, taking cuttings, or root division; the best soils for growing the herbs; how to feed, water, and generally care for them; and the most useful plans for incorporating them into garden beds. I studied the book at night, carried it to work in the morning, took it into the greenhouses, propped it up for reference on our seeding and transplanting benches, pored over it in my mother's kitchen at lunchtime, and took it home again at night. Mrs. Cashmore's copy became so dog-eared and soiled that I was at some pains to locate another copy, in good condition, to return to her.

Rosetta Clarkson came to my rescue yet again several years later, in the form of *Magic Gardens*. By now my business was devoted almost entirely to growing herbs; in dealing with customers at both the wholesale and retail levels, I was bombarded with questions on the lore, traditions, and customs of herbal culture and use. Originally published in 1939, *Magic Gardens* provides a comprehensive understanding of the world of herbs. Essentially, it is a collection of the pieces Rosetta had written for *The Herb Journal*, a periodical she and her husband, Ralph P. Clarkson, a patent attorney and journalist, had founded in 1931. I felt privileged to be invited to write the foreword to the book when it was reissued in 1992.

While I'm passing out book awards, I should also mention *The Home Garden Book of Herbs and Spices* by Milo Miloradovich, first published in 1952, which I consulted regularly as I developed our herb business, and the excellent *Rodale's Illustrated Encyclopedia of Herbs*, published in 1987.

If my own book can inform and inspire herb gardeners to the degree these earlier titles have done, I will be, as Rosetta Clarkson might say, lifted out of the hurrying present.

Four Facts of Herb Life

BEFORE WE CONSIDER the first herb garden, let's analyze the general conditions that determine how individual herbs grow. Each herb's *life cycle*, *climate requirements*, *growth pattern*, and *means of propagation* dictate what you can and can't do for it in the garden. Becoming familiar with these key factors is really more important, at this point, than knowing which names belong to which herbs.

Life Cycle

Herbs live according to one of three distinctly different timetables: annual, perennial, or biennial.

An *annual* is any plant that can be sown from seed and will mature to harvest stage within one growing season. Left outside into winter, both plant and root structure will be killed by freezing temperatures or even a light frost.

Many of our most familiar culinary herbs are annuals—basil, chervil, coriander, dill, summer savory.

A *perennial* is a plant that comes back every spring. The plant itself may be killed by frost, but the root structure is hardy and, after hibernating for the winter, it sends up new shoots at the start of spring. Mints, thyme, tarragon, sage, and oregano are all hardy perennials.

Tender perennials, such as rosemary, bay, and lemon verbena, can withstand a frost but not substantial freezing, so for practical purposes they must be either treated as annuals in the garden or brought indoors in pots over the winter months, then returned to the garden in the spring.

A *biennial* is a plant that takes 2 years to mature. Its root structure survives the first winter it spends outdoors, but when the plant goes to seed in the second growing season, it has outlived its usefulness. Parsley is the most familiar of the relatively few biennial plants.

Climate Requirements

Life cycle and climate obviously are interrelated. Because all annuals are killed by frost, they are classified as tender. But some annual herbs are more tender than others. A windy, 40°F night will kill basil but not affect the dill plant right next to it. Both are annuals, but basil is very tender and dill is not.

Most perennials are hardy, but some don't survive the winter intact because their root structures die in severe cold weather. One of my customers manages to keep her rosemary alive through the winter only because the plant is located in front of the vent for her clothes dryer, and this particular woman does a lot of laundry.

The other side of the coin is that some perennials, like French tarragon, don't do well in the *absence* of a cold winter. In similar fashion, many roses and perennial spring bulbs fail to thrive in southern gardens because the weather doesn't permit them to go dormant and recoup their energies. Plants in southern gardens also are susceptible to more damage from insects and, due to humidity, fungus.

Sunlight is important to all herbs to varying degrees. Some will tolerate partial shade, but few will really do well in total shade for long. Most herbs, which after all originated in Mediterranean countries, achieve their best growth in full sun. It is the long hours of sunlight that force the herbs to produce the oils that give them their unique aromas and flavors in the first place.

Rate and Pattern of Growth

Knowing the size, shape, and spreading pattern of each herb is indispensable to a successful garden plan. Think of herb gardening as landscape architecture practiced on a small scale. Each herb must be located to complement its neighbors and not get in the others' way. Illustrations accompanying this chapter depict the growth patterns, above and below ground, of eight representative herb plants.

Perennials must be given more room from the start, because they are permanent garden residents which grow larger every year.

Some perennials grow on a single stem, others via an underground network of roots and new shoots. It is the latter—the spreading perennials—that must be watched carefully, and periodically dug up and divided to keep them within bounds. A single mint plant left untended in good growing conditions will spread 5' in every direction within 3 years.

You must also consider an individual herb's potential for growing tall or wide, aboveground. Herbs such as angelica, lovage, or Jerusalem artichoke, which reach 6' in height, should be located at the back of the garden so they won't cast shade over shorter plants. Rosemary will grow 4' wide over a period of years if it is provided adequate protection from winter's rigors. Other herbs may be kept in place by cutting them back periodically.

Some herbs, such as parsley or chives, grow effectively in rows, and others, such as *Teucrium* (germander) and *Santolina*, can be trained into low hedges; for example, in formal knot gardens.

Certain herbs have an almost freakish rate of growth. Borage plants will crowd out their neighbors in a matter of weeks in early spring if you haven't allocated enough space to them. Bee balm and lemon verbena start slowly in the spring but bush out dramatically in summer if left untended.

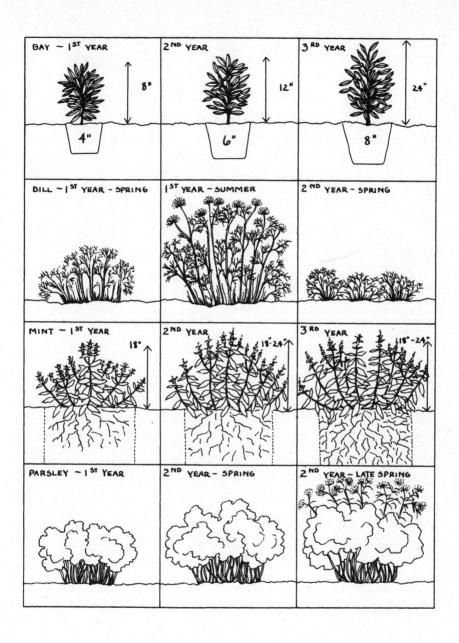

BAY ~ 1ST YEAR   8"   4"

2ND YEAR   12"   6"

3RD YEAR   24"   8"

DILL ~ 1ST YEAR - SPRING

1ST YEAR - SUMMER

2ND YEAR - SPRING

MINT ~ 1ST YEAR   18"

2ND YEAR   18"-24"

3RD YEAR   18"-24"

PARSLEY ~ 1ST YEAR

2ND YEAR - SPRING

2ND YEAR - LATE SPRING

Four Facts of Herb Life

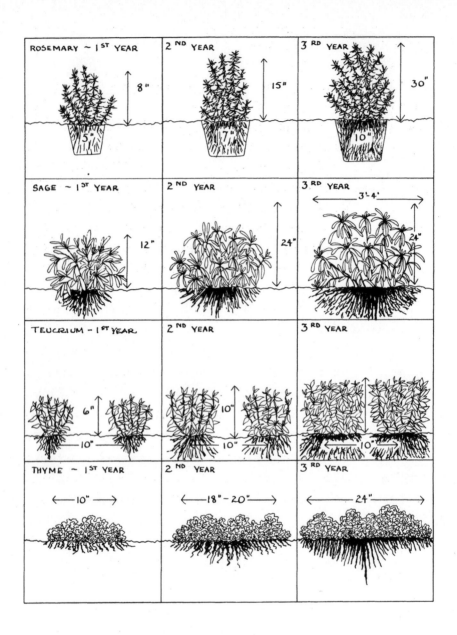

Means of Propagation

The four proven ways to coax new herbs into life are from seed sown by the gardener, from cuttings of stems or branches, from divisions of root systems, or from seed dropped by the plant itself (self-sowing).

Most annuals are started from seed, a relatively easy method. These herbs can be sown directly into the designated area in the garden or planted as seedlings after having been started from seed in planting pots or trays indoors. This indirect sowing method is useful in northern climates to get a jump on the season.

Some perennials can also be started from seed, but it is easier, with single-stemmed perennials, to take cuttings off an existing healthy plant and place the branch in a sand/perlite mixture. Properly watered and given enough light, this shoot will send out new roots in a short while.

It is even easier to propagate spreading perennials, such as those in the mint family. By digging up the root system of an established plant, one can divide the roots into as many new plants as needed.

Finally, there are the herbs that produce their own seed in the course of the growing season and, with a little luck, sow their seed in and around the area of the original plant. Annuals, such as dill, and perennials, such as oregano or lemon balm, commonly produce these so-called volunteers, which make their appearance in the garden the following spring, and invariably prompt at least one customer a year to run into our garden center declaring, "Sal, my dill's a perennial!"

II.

Building the First Garden

IN THIS SECTION we'll concentrate on developing a basic herb garden containing fifteen popular culinary herbs, planting and cultivating them in a sunny 8' x 8' area.

A garden of modest dimensions can be built in a matter of hours, yet easily expanded in subsequent years if desired. The trouble with starting too big, or with too elaborate a design in mind, is that you may not get the project off the ground, or you'll do it in slipshod fashion. Or, you'll end up with an area that's really too large for your present interests, needs, or abilities. Herb gardening is supposed to be pleasurable and relatively carefree, not a burden, so set your sights small at the start.

I have chosen an 8' x 8' garden plan because it is a manageable space in which to create a raised bed for the herbs. A garden bed raised 12" to 20" above surrounding land will provide the herbs with the well-drained soil they need to thrive.

The value of good drainage was brought home to me dramatically one year when I visited a six-acre commercial planting of tarragon in Ohio. The soil in the fields seemed almost bone dry, but when I dug up a couple of plants, I saw they had lush and complex root systems. My farmer friend explained, "Our place looks flat, but the soil level is elevated, and we enjoy great drainage." Even if the field had been heavily watered, by rainfall or irrigation, the ground would have absorbed the moisture and allowed the plants to send out their roots aggressively.

There are other benefits of a raised bed. Such a garden is often aesthetically more pleasing, standing apart from its surroundings. The eye is drawn to an elevated garden as to a centerpiece on a table. A raised bed is easier to tend and cultivate. With a raised bed of proper soil tilth and consistency, water and wetness won't impede root growth in the herb plants.

Raised Bed Architecture

An easy way to achieve elevated growing areas is to build perimeters for them with safe, durable materials. Any weather-resistant material that provides a solid means of elevating and containing the garden space will do the job. It can be 2" x 12" cedar or similar hardwood planks; logs of white oak, fir, juniper, or locust; some variation on the fiber-plastic building materials that have become available in recent years; or even concrete blocks. I have seen my customers frame their raised beds with all kinds of makeshift materials, from recycled barn beams to dismantled sandboxes and old diving boards. These improvised gardens may strike traditionalists as eccentric, but if the herbs don't mind, neither should we. One caveat: avoid making barriers from railroad ties or utility poles that have been treated with creosote, which may leach into the soil to harmful effect. A friend of mine in the garden business once stained all the wood benches in one of his greenhouses with creosote. The fumes killed $5,000 worth of his houseplants.

A raised bed can be built without perimeter materials of any kind simply by adding soil to the 8' x 8' area to a height of 12" to 20". In some of our garden plans, you will see that pathways have been introduced into the raised bed, to give gardeners greater access to their plants and also to facilitate drainage. Garden paths are of course an indispensable design element to the romantic impulse within many gardeners.

The Soil Bed

Creating the right soil mix in the raised bed—soil, compost, and peat moss in equal amounts, plus some perlite—means spending a little money at the garden center, feed store, or nursery, but it will be worth the investment. For under $200, you can fill an 8' x 8' area to a depth of 12" to 20" with the following plant-friendly ingredients:

- **Topsoil** (30 percent) as the basic growing medium for the herbs.
- **Compost** (30 percent) to provide the "breakfast of champions" nutrients for the herbs, and to engender good tilth, or texture, in the soil.
- **Peat moss** (30 percent) to condition the mix by loosening the soil and blending with it. (You could use sphagnum moss instead of peat moss, but it is more expensive in some areas, and its coarser character makes it a bit harder to incorporate into the soil mix.)
- **Perlite**, crushed volcanic matter, or pumice (10 percent) to lighten the soil. (You could use vermiculite instead of perlite, but this cork-like matter derived from mica tends to retain moisture, which is not so good for most herbs, so I definitely favor the perlite.)

You may buy these materials if your soil is poor or claylike or if you're constructing the garden on top of an existing lawn area. In the latter case, you should also be sure to break up the sod with a grub ax or spade and turn it grass-side down before filling in the area with the topsoil, compost, peat moss, and perlite. Once these ingredients have been thoroughly blended with a spade fork, the soil should be tested for its degree of acidity or alkalinity. Generally, most herbs do best in very slightly acid soil with a 6.0 to 6.5 pH reading. Dill, basil, and parsley benefit in a slightly sweeter soil, but it's not essential to add lime in those spots to get a decent crop. Your Cooperative Extension Service (see Sources, page 238) will analyze a sample of your soil for a small fee.

The fifteen herbs I recommend for the first garden all have practical value in the kitchen. Also, taken together, growing them happens to involve virtually every trick or technique for growing practically all the herbs. They are, in the order in which we present them:

chives

sweet marjoram

thyme

basil

coriander

chervil

parsley

dill

summer savory

mint

oregano

tarragon

sage

rosemary

bay

The most convenient way to get this first garden going is to buy all fifteen herbs as established plants and simply transplant them to your prepared soil bed. Years ago, few garden centers or nurseries offered herb plants, except perhaps for parsley and chives. Nowadays, all fifteen herbs are readily available and reasonably priced—$3 to $5 for plants in 4" pots.

If you choose this shortcut to success in building your first herb garden, you must still exercise caution in choosing the dates you plant the herbs in the ground. The transplanting may be done as early as one month prior to your spring frost day for the hardy plants among these herbs:

chives
sweet marjoram
thyme
parsley
mint
oregano
tarragon
sage

The tender herbs should not be placed outdoors until all danger of frost is past in your gardening zone. These are:

coriander
chervil
dill
summer savory
rosemary and bay (tender perennials)

And wait yet another 2 weeks to plant the ultra-sensitive:

basil

You may locate the herbs within the garden area any way you like, within reason. The plan on page 100 suggests one possible arrangement. It is not completely arbitrary, for "the four facts of herbal life" influenced the design, specifically as follows:

All the spreading perennials—sweet marjoram, mint, oregano, and tarragon—have been given relatively more space in which to grow than the other herbs.

The shorter-growing herbs—thyme, chervil, and parsley—have been placed in the front or on the edge of the garden, and the tallest-growing herbs—dill, tarragon, and coriander—are in the back.

Two additional features are worthy of note, though not apparent in the plan itself—because they're underground.

The mint, most rampant grower of the spreading perennials, should be physically boxed in below the soil line to prevent its growth beyond reasonable limits in the future. Remember, mint likes to run away from home more than any other herb. So, take a large 14" to 16" plastic container that you once brought home—perhaps with a new dwarf apple tree sapling in it—cut out its bottom, and sink it into the soil bed where you want to locate the mint. In this confined growing area, your mint will thrive without crowding its neighbors.

The bay and rosemary should be planted in clay pots buried at soil level. That's because, as tender perennials, eventually they will require protection from the cold, at least wherever winter temperatures fall below 20°F. Keeping these two herbs in pots makes them much easier to move to a sunny indoor spot in the late fall. This method also keeps root systems from spreading so much. If you planted your bay and rosemary without pots, the plants would develop deep tap roots that you would have to sever in order to pot them up in the fall, and they would have filled out so much that you'd need unmanageably large pots to handle them.

The one drawback to keeping bay and rosemary in pots in the garden is that the plants will tend to dry out more quickly, so they must be watched carefully and watered more often during droughts.

Starting from Scratch

AS I SAID EARLIER, the easiest way to get started in herb gardening is to buy all the herb plants you need, install them in your raised bed, and stand back to watch them flourish. If in fact you decide to take this approach, you can skip the following few chapters on propagation.

However, if you are really interested in becoming a soil-stained, keen-for-green herb gardener of the first order, I encourage you to start from scratch, without the advantage of established plants acquired from a professional grower. This more challenging path has one great advantage: it will make you familiar with the techniques for growing all herbs, in a way that starting your garden from established plants would not.

I also think that if you focus on learning to grow the fifteen basic cooking herbs, you'll emerge a much better all-around gardener than if you try to absorb cultural information about hundreds of herbs in mind-boggling alphabetical order (as they are frequently presented).

We'll discuss the basic herbs in five sets of three. Each threesome happens to involve a different technique or somewhat different conditions for successful growing. Remember, once you've learned to grow these fifteen herbs, you'll know how to grow most other herbs with just a minimum of additional information. So it's worth taking the time and trouble to cultivate those fifteen herbs correctly.

The indoor sowing activities to be described commence about 3 months before the average date of the last frost in the spring in your neck of the woods. You can determine this date for your locale by asking the U.S. Cooperative Extension Service or a knowledgeable local source, such as your garden center. For example, in my area of Connecticut, May 15 has been statistically determined to be the last day we're likely to get a frost. So in this area, February 15 would be the time to sow the first group of herbs indoors.

A certain amount of indoor sowing is a necessity up north. If we waited until the soil was warm enough to sow the seed directly outdoors, in many cases no crop of any significance would develop before the end of our short growing season.

Indoor sowing also makes sense simply because so many of the herb seeds are tiny. Outdoors they can be crushed or kicked or washed away. Indoors they can be nurtured into life under proper supervision.

It's a good idea to stick to the timing suggested for sowing the various seeds indoors. The slow-growing herbs need all the time stipulated in order to develop properly. And the ones that grow quickly get leggy if kept inside beyond their time. Keep them all on schedule (see the Start from Scratch Schedule on pages 236–237 for precise planting dates), and you'll have healthy plants to put into the garden when the time comes.

What You'll Need to Start Herbs from Seed Indoors

INDOOR SOWING OF HERBS in small quantities doesn't take much room at all, but there are certain materials, devices, methods, and conditions that will help ensure success. I'll describe them here briefly before getting into the sowing and growing of the specific herbs.

Southern exposure. The best location in the home for developing herb seedlings is a window with a sunny southern exposure—one that is exposed to sunlight all day long in the winter. If you can set your pots and trays on the windowsill or a table at this location, you should be able to develop the herbs properly. A shelf or table area that is 3' long and 6" to 9" wide, positioned directly alongside this window, will give you all the space you need.

If your best window is oriented somewhat southwest or southeast, you won't get as much of the sunlight available and your seedlings will tend to lean in the direction of the missing sun. That simply means you'll have to rotate the plants every 3 or 4 days to keep them growing reasonably straight.

Calculate the amount of sunlight your best window gets before you begin sowing—say, in mid-February. If the sun shines into that window for 7 to 8 hours, you're sitting pretty. You could get away with a little less light before germination, but after the seeds have sprouted the 8-hour exposure is essential. Without it the plants will grow weak and spindly very quickly.

If your most convenient window doesn't attract the minimum sunlight required, you can make up for it by using fluorescent lights. For every hour of the required natural sunlight your site misses, expose the plants to 2 hours of fluorescent light. For example, if your window receives only 6 hours of sun, add 4 hours of fluorescent light, which in total is the equivalent of about 8 hours of natural sunlight.

Temperature. The best temperature for developing healthy herb plants indoors is 70°F before germination and 60 to 65°F after germination. The need to conserve energy has lowered average household temperatures somewhat in recent years, so more homes now have the correct range for herbs.

You can create a higher temperature if necessary by covering the pots with shrink-wrap or a thin sheet of polyethylene plastic tacked to a simple frame. This will increase the temperature by 5 to 10 degrees, help retain moisture greenhouse-style, and so stimulate much better germination. Be sure to remove the plastic once sprouting occurs.

Seed. Some herb seeds are available on seed racks in retail locations in early spring, but there are not as many to choose from as can be found online or in print seed catalogs. It will be easier, and possibly cheaper, to get what you want by ordering from a reputable seed house. (See Sources, page 238.) Order the seed in December or early January to ensure that it reaches you with time to spare. One seed packet of each herb will be more than enough for your first garden. About 90 to 100 seeds come in a packet for most varieties. This varies with each supplier, and also from year to year within the same seed house. In recent years the trend has been to include fewer and fewer seeds. Anyway, you'll need only about a fourth of the seed for the first year. The rest is insurance against an extremely low germination rate—or an accident, such as the cat knocking over the whole project.

Planting mix. The soil-compost-peat moss-perlite mixture described earlier for the outdoor soil bed is indispensable for indoor sowing. A bag of commercial potting soil should be your source of the soil part of the formula for convenience and also because, unlike your garden soil, it is already sterilized and completely screened to be free of stones and other impediments.

Don't underestimate the importance of starting with the right mix to sow the seeds in. I'm so convinced of its value that I've started bagging the blend in small quantities for my own customers. Please don't make the mistake, as so many novice gardeners have done, of trying to start herb seeds in any of the various commercial planting mixes available, such as "herb seed kits" especially those containing vermiculite. These mixes are not really designed with herbs in mind. None of them will drain quickly enough for growing some of the more delicate varieties. I spend half the month of March looking at customers' dead or dying seedlings that they have tried to grow in such mixes.

Cutting mix. We recommend growing certain herbs not from seed, but from cuttings—small branches snipped off of an existing plant. Placed in the proper rooting mixture, these cuttings eventually send out roots and become established as new plants. The best rooting medium for these cuttings consists of one part sand, one part perlite, and one part peat moss. You'll have these ingredients on hand already if you've acquired what you need for the ideal planting mix already mentioned. We eliminate the soil and compost from the cutting mix to improve drainage to the maximum, because cuttings are extremely susceptible to many fungus problems.

Play sand. A small bag of this fine clean sand (readily available in hardware stores or toy stores) will be more than enough for your needs. The trick is to sprinkle a thin layer of the play sand over the herb seed after you have made your sowing. The sand is heavy enough to keep the tiny, buoyant seeds in their place during the germination period. And it is fine enough to drain quickly, so that after sprouting the herb seedlings will not have too much moisture around the base of their stems, so they will not be likely to perish from damping-off—a fungus-produced rotting of the tender new shoot above the soil line, which is the number one problem immediately after germination. Basil, dill, and sage are particularly susceptible to damping-off.

Planting pots. If you have any gardening experience at all, you probably have various containers handy already, or you can improvise with confidence. If you're a rank beginner, you should acquire a half dozen 3- to 4-inch-diameter clay pots (plastic pots are less desirable because they're not as porous and so may retain moisture too long). That's all you'll need for the indoor sowing project.

When the time comes, fill the pots with your planting mix. Make sure the mix is level and slightly damp. If it is bone dry, sprinkle it thoroughly 24 hours before sowing. It should not be soggy wet when it's time to receive the seed.

A container for the container. It's much easier to control the indoor sowing project if all your working pots and trays can be held in one larger leak-proof tray or box. This is not an absolute necessity, but later on it will make it easy for you to put all your young seedlings outside on the odd balmy early spring day. More important, it can be used effectively to prevent any of the herbs from standing in water, a condition that quickly promotes rot in an herb plant's roots. The trick is to cover the bottom of your container with a layer of pebbles. That way, when you do irrigate, any excess water will drain through the bottom of the pots and out of contact with the root systems—which will have developed all the way down to the bottom of the pots toward the end of their time indoors.

Mister. For use before germination. This could be a converted spray bottle originally containing a household cleaner. Once you have thoroughly washed and rinsed it, you can fill it with lukewarm water and use it for keeping the planting mix moist during the germination period without disrupting the soil or dislodging the tiny seeds, as might happen if you irrigated with a conventional watering can or, God forbid, submitted your pots and trays to a cascade under the kitchen faucet. Many growers submerge the seeded pots in water for several minutes and allow the medium to absorb the water from the bottom. This is an effective procedure, but it's probably too time-consuming for most people—and also too messy for most kitchen sinks and bathtubs.

Watering can. For use after germination. Any manageably small indoor-type watering can will do.

Fertilizer. The herb seedlings will require one small dose of fertilizer at a certain stage in their development. I recommend using a natural or organic type fertilizer, such as fish emulsion or liquid seaweed. This is what we use in our greenhouses, and it works fine. The small amount you'll need won't cost much. Nowadays you can find a wide range of organic fertilizers in seed catalogs and at most garden centers. Or you can fertilize with skim milk instead of water. I've used skim milk successfully on herb seedlings in their early stages. It really promotes healthy growth—unless your cat gets into it.

Insect repellent. Herbs are not bug-attractive; in fact, they are frequently used in vegetable patches by organic gardeners because they tend to keep bugs away. Even in greenhouses, where insects can be a real problem, our herbs stay relatively insect-free. Your houseplants are much more likely to harbor insects than your herb plants. If you have a lot of houseplants, watch more carefully for bugs migrating to your herbs.

If, despite all that, you notice insect activity, a good way to get rid of it fast is to mix up a batch of something known in my family as "Nana's Bug Juice." Put a couple of cloves of garlic and some cayenne pepper in a half cup of water or cider vinegar and pour into a blender. (You may want to dedicate an old blender for this purpose.) Mix the ingredients thoroughly, then pour them through a piece of cheesecloth or some other filtering device so that you end up with a clear solution. Pour this into your mister and then spray the affected plants.

This spray will work at least as well as any chemical spray and won't coat your plants with anything poisonous or unpalatable. These herbs are food crops, of course, and people are always plucking their leaves to taste them. With this in mind, you're more likely to take a strictly nonchemical approach, as I do, to growing herbs. Insecticidal soaps, available in small spray bottles, also chase away bugs; many of these products have been certified by authorities on organic growing techniques.

Cooling-off place. This is required to expose the herb plants to cooler outdoor temperatures before finally setting them out in the garden. A cold frame is ideal, but an unheated room or sun porch with good light is almost as effective. If you don't have either, then set the plants outside for a few hours on warm days when the time comes; only be sure to protect them from the harsh winds that are so common in early spring. A windbreak of plastic that surrounds the plants on three sides will prevent the wind from setting the herbs back.

Pad and pencil. It's a good idea to maintain at least an informal journal of your herb-growing activities. If you note down when you sowed each herb, when sprouts first appeared, and so on, you'll perform the later steps in handling each herb at the right time and with more confidence generally, and you'll be much better prepared when next year rolls around.

Cluster Sowing Indoors

Group 1: Chives ✦ Sweet Marjoram ✦ Thyme

Now let's go through our methods for growing the fifteen most desirable culinary herbs.

The way to start the first group of chives, sweet marjoram, and thyme indoors is by cluster sowing. This means evenly sprinkling the seed across the planting surface of a 4" pot, then covering it with play sand and misting daily until germination.

Use clay pots rather than peat pots for this group. The plants will be in pots for a long period of time, so porous clay will help control the moisture level in the soil mix. Also, chives and marjoram have heavy root systems that benefit from confinement. They wouldn't be as happy in a biodegradable pot, because developing root systems grow into the pot itself, making transplanting more stressful for the plant.

Figure on using 10 to 20 seeds of marjoram and thyme per pot, but be more generous with the chives—say 20 to 30 seeds—as chives develop best in clumps.

1. Sow seeds evenly in clay pots.
2. Cover with fine sand and label.
3. Mist daily until germination.
4. After germination, water as needed.
5. Fertilize 2 weeks after germination.
6. Acclimatize in cold frame or on back porch.
7. Transplant out of pot into garden.
8. Shelter with plastic container.

The chive seed will be easy to handle because it's flat and at least five times bigger than the sweet marjoram or thyme seed. You can shake it out of the seed package with good control. Take an extra minute, though, to sow the smaller seeds from between your fingertips. Make sure the thyme and marjoram seeds fall where you want them to grow so they won't crowd each other out later on. Inexpensive hand seed sowers, available in some seed catalogs, make it a cinch to sow seeds of any size in a controlled fashion.

Cluster sowing allows all three herbs to grow in a fairly thick stand and so creates a stronger unit for moving into the garden, and this gives you much more productivity in the first year.

You couldn't sow most vegetables this way, but these herb plants don't have the high nutritional needs that would make them compete with each other and eventually suffer in such limited space. The grouping of chive, sweet marjoram, and thyme plants that should emerge in each 4" pot will all do fine.

If you sow only 2 or 3 seeds, rather than a cluster of them, in each pot, it will take much longer for these perennials to spread enough to give you plenty to pick from for the kitchen. With these particular herbs, you can get there faster by cluster sowing.

Thyme and sweet marjoram take 4 to 5 days to germinate, chives about 7 days.

During this pregermination period, the pots should be kept in natural light but preferably not in full direct sunlight. If there's a chance they'll sprout in full sun when you're out of the house for a couple of days, cover the seedbed with a piece of cheesecloth or burlap. That will keep the seedlings from withering away before you get back.

Mist the pots every morning until shoots appear, to keep the soil moist— but without creating flood conditions.

After germination, start using the watering can, but do so carefully, irrigating only when the soil surface is dry to the touch, only in the mornings, and only at the base of the plants, keeping water off the stems and leaves of the seedlings as best you can.

Herb Gardening from the Ground Up

Fertilize with liquid fish emulsion or skim milk about 2 weeks after germination. Fill a watering can and dissolve the fertilizer in the water according to the proportions given on the label. One shot of the extra food—about ½ cup per pot—is all the seedlings will need to get firmly established. If you water them with this solution, you'll give the plants the correct amount of food. If you're going to use skim milk instead of fertilizer, just "water" with skim milk.

In another month, the herbs will be ready to go into the garden. At this time the chives should be about 6" high and the lower-growing thyme and sweet marjoram about 4" high. If they get much taller than this, and it is still too soon to safely put them out in the garden, simply cut them back to 2" high and use the clippings in the kitchen. Cutting the seedlings back makes the plants stronger.

Being hardy perennials, chives, marjoram, and thyme are resistant to frost; that's why they can go into the garden a month *before* the last frost date in the spring. However, because these plants have never had the experience of being outdoors, it's a good idea to introduce them to conditions in the real world gradually during the last week before transplanting them. This can be done by setting them out in your cooling-off place. Then, when the time comes to knock the soil ball out of each pot and plant it intact in the garden, the herbs will accept the transfer without complaint. This hardening-off process is very important for giving an extra level of protection to the vulnerable young plants.

If, after they have been set out, there is unusually cold weather, with subfreezing temperatures predicted, the herbs will be happier under some temporary protection. Clear plastic half-gallon or gallon containers with the necks cut out are well-suited for this purpose. Put a stone on top to prevent wind from blowing the containers over.

Spot Sowing Indoors

Group 2: Basil ✦ Chervil ✦ Coriander

Unlike the preceding three herbs, basil, chervil, and coriander are all *tender*. They can't be put out in the garden until after all danger of frost is past. Therefore, you should start these from seed indoors about a month after you've started the chives, marjoram, and thyme. Then they won't spend too much time waiting.

1. Spot sow seeds in peat pots.
2. Cover with fine sand and label.
3. Mist daily until germination.
4. After germination, water as needed.
5. Thin the basil, leaving the single healthiest plant.
6. Fertilize with fish emulsion.
7. Acclimatize in cold frame or back porch.
8. Transplant to garden in peat pots; shelter if necessary.

This group of herbs can be started the same way you started chives, marjoram, and thyme, with one big difference. Instead of sprinkling a dozen seeds as you did for each perennial, sow *only 4 to 6 seeds per pot* for the basil, chervil, and coriander. When the basil seedlings have grown about 1" to 2" high, pluck out all but the single healthiest plant from each pot. For the chervil and coriander, leave the cluster of emerging seedlings as is.

Use peat pots for this group if possible. Because you're starting them later, you don't have to worry about the pot disintegrating before the plants are ready to go into the garden. Also, because their root systems are more delicate than those of most herbs, they can be protected from disturbance simply by planting them, pot and all. This couldn't be done if you had used a clay or plastic pot.

Just to make it absolutely clear, what follows is the spot sowing method, step by step:

Fill 4" pots with your planting mix and make sure the mix is level and reasonably moist. Sow 4 to 6 seeds of each variety in its own pot. Cover the seed with fine sand. Label the pots with the name of each herb to prevent mix-ups later.

Place the pots in a well-lighted place and mist every day until sprouts appear, which should be in about 1 week.

After germination, keep providing good light and water carefully as needed.

In 2 to 3 weeks, when the seedlings are approximately 2" high, thin the basil to just one plant per pot. Be sure to save the healthiest—the seedling with the greenest color and thickest stem. When you weed out the rejects, protect the seedling of choice by gently pressing down on the soil around it with two fingers.

In about a week, fertilize lightly with liquid fish emulsion or skim milk. Continue watering as needed. In another 3 weeks the basil, chervil, and coriander should have reached a height of 4" to 6".

At this point the seedlings are just about ready for setting out into the garden. First, though, acclimate them to outdoor conditions for a few days in your cooling-off place—especially the basil, the most tender of the herbs. Even with temperatures in the 50s, a 15- to 20-mph wind could hurt it. To be on the safe side, don't put it out into the garden until about 2 weeks after your last spring frost date.

Plant the herbs where you want them in your garden, peat pots and all. Bury the pot rims below soil too, so they don't act like wicks and cause moisture to evaporate from the soil. Or simply break off the rims so that no pots are above the soil line.

Use those recycled plastic containers to act as shields for the young plants should the weather turn cold.

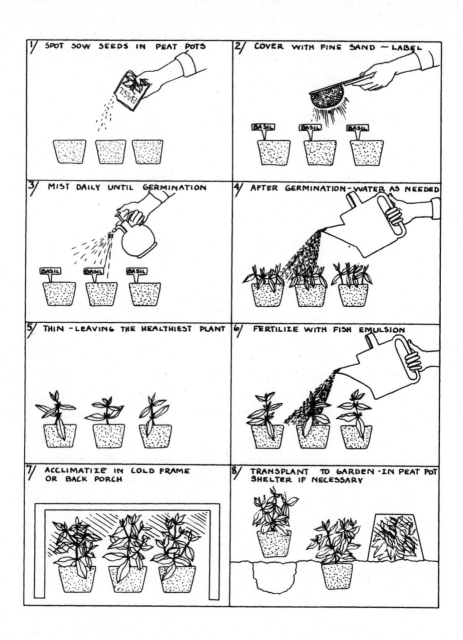

Herb Gardening from the Ground Up

Cluster and Row
Sowing Outdoors

Group 3: Parsley + Summer Savory + Dill

You can sow this group directly outdoors, because the herbs will develop fast enough after sprouting to give you a good crop by the end of the summer. But wait until at least the last spring frost date to make these sowings.

The illustration on page 56 shows our technique for sowing these herbs in clusters in the garden. You can also sow the herbs directly in the garden in straight rows—some gardeners find rows of plants easier to maintain and harvest.

1. Prepare bed and warm soil with cardboard frame and plastic wrap cover.
2. Sow seeds in warmed spots.
3. Cover with fine sand, then water.
4. Replace plastic wrap cover.
5. Remove plastic wrap cover after germination.
6. Remove cardboard frame when seedlings are 2" tall.

Here's a trick for creating a planting site for each herb that will warm up the soil for quicker germination, protect each area from the elements before and after germination, and keep your sowing areas clearly marked so you don't step on them by mistake in the early stages. About 2 or 3 days *before* you plan to sow your seed, prepare and level the soil in the spots you've selected for each of the three herbs within your garden area. Cut up an empty

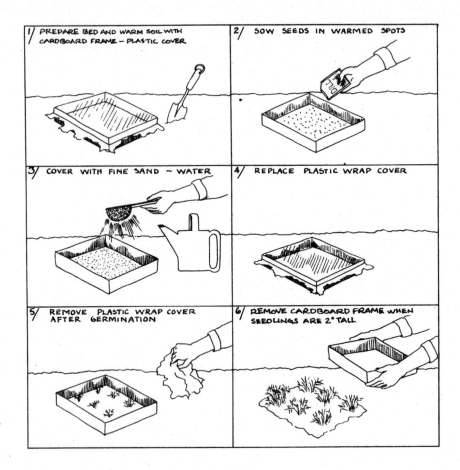

1/ PREPARE BED AND WARM SOIL WITH CARDBOARD FRAME – PLASTIC COVER	2/ SOW SEEDS IN WARMED SPOTS
3/ COVER WITH FINE SAND – WATER	4/ REPLACE PLASTIC WRAP COVER
5/ REMOVE PLASTIC WRAP COVER AFTER GERMINATION	6/ REMOVE CARDBOARD FRAME WHEN SEEDLINGS ARE 2" TALL

cardboard carton into 3"-high temporary frames, one for each of the sowing areas. Then cover each frame with a patch of clear plastic wrap—you can even use plastic sandwich bags secured around each frame with rubber bands.

Sink the frames 1" into the soil—deep enough to make them secure—at the chosen sites.

The soil inside these three miniature greenhouses will warm up much faster than the soil in the rest of the garden. In a couple of days it'll be ready to receive your seeds.

On the day of sowing, remove the plastic and sprinkle, by hand or using a hand seed sower, 10 to 20 seeds of each herb in each of the selected areas, then cover with fine sand. Water thoroughly before replacing the plastic cover.

During the germination period, the clear plastic tops will let the sunlight come through and keep the soil bed warm while preventing any hard spring rain from creating havoc.

Sprouts should appear in 5 days for the dill and summer savory, and not for 2 weeks for the more methodical parsley. When there are sprouts in all sown areas, remove the plastic. After the plants are well established—say 2" high—remove the cardboard carton frame as well. You don't need to thin unless you have an exceptionally thick stand from oversowing.

Test sowing of herb seed. Though it's not really necessary if you have fresh seed from a reputable supplier, you could test sow the parsley, summer savory, and dill indoors at the same time you're toiling over the earlier groups. Test sowing is definitely advisable if you're working with leftover seed from previous years. Fill a 5" x 7" container with your soil mix and make three shallow furrows. Sow 10 seeds of each herb per row. Then cover with fine sand and mist every day until germination. Now count the sprouts. If you get 7 or 8 out of 10 seeds to germinate in each row it means the seed is good. When the time comes for sowing outdoors, you can be confident you'll get good results. Anything below 50 percent germination means you're going to have to sow more seed, when the time comes, to get the thick stand of plants you want. If you get only 20 to 30 percent germination, throw the package out and find a new supplier before your spring sowing date.

In any case, don't throw out the seedlings from your test sowing. Harvest them for use in a salad.

Making Divisions of Spreading Perennials

Group 4: Mint ✦ Tarragon ✦ Oregano

The best way to start these three perennials in your garden, when you can't buy them, is to divide established plants from somebody else's garden.

Actually, you can also start mint and oregano from seed, but it is much easier to get them from a division, which amounts to Instant Plant. Mint is a little tricky—it takes a long time to germinate. Furthermore, spearmint and peppermint grown from seed do not have the desirable mint flavor. Only mint grown from root division will flavor your mint juleps properly.

1. Dig out entire plant in early spring when growth is just showing.
2. Divide mint: use a spade fork to loosen and separate a clump.
3. Divide oregano: cut out a "plug" with a trowel or spade.
4. Divide tarragon: holding two old stems, pull apart.
5. Replace original plant firmly and water.
6. Plant the division and water.

It's very hard to find the right seed for true oregano—I mean the genuine, pizza-quality oregano, as opposed to the bland pot marjoram variety or "wild marjoram" that is often passed off as the real thing. Actually, even if you had harvested your own seed from an oregano plant of proven tastiness, often something would be lost in the succeeding plant generations, and it wouldn't have the distinctive oregano flavor.

In my own garden, at least, this appears to be the fault of the bees, who commute indiscriminately between oregano blossoms in one part of the garden and pot marjoram blossoms in another. I suspect that the resulting cross-pollination is what adulterates the oregano seed later on. Anyway, that's why, when I want to start new oregano plants, I always prefer to make divisions or cuttings from the bona fide plants.

As for true French tarragon, it does not produce seed, so there's nothing to sow. Russian tarragon produces seed, so that is what is offered in some herb seed catalogs. But it has such a bland flavor that it doesn't belong in the basic culinary gardens.

The French tarragon, like oregano, may also be started from a cutting, according to a method I'll describe shortly for the last group of herbs. However, it's much easier to propagate the plant by division, and that's why I place it in this group.

The time to make divisions of perennial herbs is when they first begin to show life again in the new season—approximately 4 to 6 weeks before the last spring frost date. At this time you can hack away at each plant without seriously hampering life and growth potential. These perennials that spread by meandering root systems underground actually benefit by periodic division, for the operation prevents them from choking on their own prolix growth pattern. This treatment also makes for a neater garden generally.

Thus early spring is the time to launch a search for friends, relatives, neighbors, and, if necessary, total strangers—anyone who has an established herb garden in the yard. You'll quickly discover that most herb gardeners are more than willing to share divisions with you, because they're usually trying to reduce or confine their perennial holdings anyway. You're really just helping them to do a bit of spring cleaning, and it's in that spirit that I suggest you offer your services.

The simplest way to obtain a division is to dig up the entire plant and then pull or tear it apart into pieces, each piece containing something from aboveground—the plant itself—and something from below ground—the root system. Each of these pieces really constitutes a new plant, and all you

1/ DIG OUT ENTIRE PLANT IN EARLY SPRING — GROWTH JUST SHOWING

2/ DIVIDE MINT — USE A SPADE FORK TO LOOSEN AND SEPARATE A CLUMP

3/ DIVIDE OREGANO — CUT OUT A "PLUG" WITH A TROWEL OR SPADE

4/ DIVIDE TARRAGON — HOLDING TWO OLD STEMS — PULL APART

5/ REPLACE ORIGINAL PLANT FIRMLY — WATER

6/ PLANT DIVISION — WATER

have to do to make it yours is plant it in your own garden. Pack it into the soil gently but firmly, and give it one good watering.

In early spring there's not enough growth aboveground to put much of a burden on any exposed root system, but by midseason, after perennials have established leafy growth, their need for water becomes critical, so don't keep them unprotected for long. If the herbs are already more than 4" to 6" tall, consider yourself tardy in making the divisions. In that case, take precautions. Before you do anything else, thoroughly water the area around the plants to be divided. After you've made your divisions, cover the exposed roots with moist soil and keep them covered in transit to their new home. After transplanting, water again. Remember, the more growth there is on top of the plant, the more important it is to keep the plant thoroughly watered until it has had a chance to re-establish itself.

Generally speaking, you should not attempt divisions of any perennials—in addition to herbs, that means peonies, phlox, or bee balm, among other ornamentals—during the feverish growing periods of June, July, and August. Roots are not supporting as much growth in early spring or early fall, so that's when you should make your move. Sometimes nature will conspire to persecute even transplants that have been moved at the proper time. Several days of unseasonably hot weather in early spring may cause the plants newly made from divisions to wilt. But all is not lost—just cut the plants back and give them time to regain their form.

Each perennial has its own peculiar growth pattern, so let me try to describe more precisely the dividing operations involved for the herbs in the present group.

Mint. This is the easiest plant to divide; if you fail at this, you have reason to sell the home grounds and move into an apartment. As soon as the sprouts appear, take a spade fork and loosen the soil around a grouping of them. Then shake the roots free of dirt and make your divisions. Be sure you have at least one sprout aboveground connected to a healthy root from below ground.

Oregano. This herb sprouts up in much tighter groupings than mint does, so it's a little harder to isolate and remove individual divisions. I would simply take a trowel or spade and carve out a grouping of the shoots. The soil and roots form a plug. If you take your plug carefully, you'll find that the herb's compact root system will hold the whole grouping together for easy removal and transplanting.

French tarragon. Dig the entire plant out of the ground as soon as the new sprouts show its location. Then shake all the soil free. This will reveal to you the octopus-like root system. Find two old stems from last year's growth and hold them firmly in each hand, then pull the whole shebang apart. Replace one half in the donor garden and save the other half for your garden. Older, more established plants with multiple stems will yield as many as 8 to 10 divisions.

Taking Cuttings of Single-Stemmed Perennials

Group 5: Sage ✦ Rosemary ✦ Bay

For a variety of reasons, these herbs are the most difficult plants for new-comers to install in their first gardens, unless they are able to buy the plants outright from a professional herb grower.

There are three ways to do it on your own, and if you're just starting in herb gardening, I would try them in the following order.

1. Take cutting with sharp knife and remove lower leaves.
2. Plant in moist 50 percent sand/50 percent perlite mix in a clay pot.
3. Mist lightly each morning.
4. Pull gently on cutting to test for root development.
5. After several weeks of root development, transplant to sand-perlite/soil-peat mixture in clay pot, and water.
6. Pinch out center stem to promote bushiness.
7. Acclimatize in cold frame or back porch.
8. Transfer to the garden, set rim of pot below soil, and water.

Alternatively, if you're an optimist, you might try cluster sowing seed of each herb in February—following the techniques already given for starting chives, marjoram, and thyme from seed. If germination is achieved, transplant the strongest seedlings to individual pots.

Compared to chives, sweet marjoram, and thyme, sage is a bit more difficult to grow from seed. Rosemary is even harder, and bay is harder still. Sage won't sprout for at least a week, rosemary for 2 weeks, and bay for 4 weeks. You may have the right soil mix and the right amount of light and moisture and still not get a good rate of germination.

So, if sowing the seed fails, option two is to locate someone who is such an advanced gardener that he or she has brought these herbs indoors for the winter. This may not be easy. Many people leave sage plants in the ground over winter because they're hardy. Also, they zealously guard their bay plants—which produce relatively sparsely in northern areas—against any tampering. Nevertheless, if you can find someone in February or March who has all three plants in fine fettle indoors, and who is willing to let you snip a small branch off of each of them, you have the means for propagating these herbs *by cutting*.

Keep in mind, though, that the people who are friendly enough to let you come into their herb gardens in spring to make divisions of spreading perennials will not necessarily let you hack away at the single-stemmed perennials they've brought indoors and carefully tended all winter long. These plants generally won't be as big or as invulnerable as the mints and such. If they think you don't look like you know what you're doing, their owners won't let you touch them.

The best way to take a cutting is to break off or cut off a new side shoot or the tip of the main stem of the established plant. Cut with a sharp clean knife, not a pair of scissors, which would tend to pinch or seal the end of the cutting and therefore make it harder for the stem to send out roots.

The bay or sage cutting need only be 2" to 3" long, with two or three leaves on it. Don't just pluck off a leaf. The rosemary cutting should be a bit longer—3" to 4". Make sure some of the soft branch is included. If it's soft and greenish, it is relatively new growth and will take favorably to rooting. If it's brown and hard—woody—don't take it, because it will be too hard to root. Of the three, the bay is most likely to have been pruned and trimmed a lot and so offers little in the way of good cuttings; just take the best you can find.

Once you have your cuttings, prepare your mix of one part sand and perlite, and one part peat moss and pack it in an appropriate porous container, such as a small clay pot or a plastic tray with holes in the bottom.

It's important to use this highly drainable sand/perlite/peat moss medium rather than your standard planting mix, because cuttings, having no root system at all, are susceptible to wet rot. Including soil, compost, or vermiculite in the mix would keep the cuttings too wet too long.

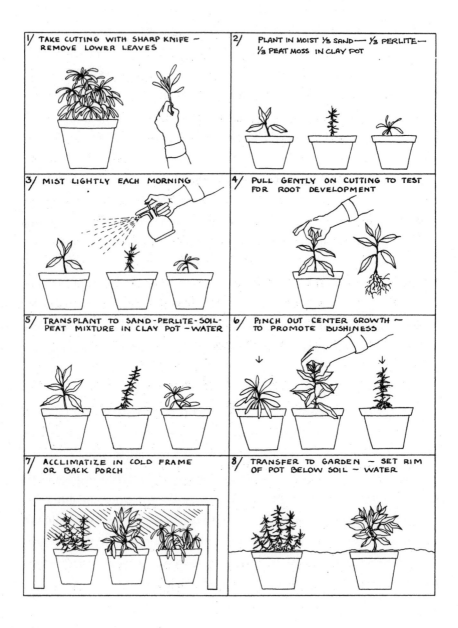

Wet the mixture and pack it down so it's good and firm. Insert the bay or sage stem ½" to 1" into the mixture so it's standing erect. The needle-like leaves of rosemary grow close together, so there may be 10 or 12 leaves on a 3" cutting. Strip the leaves on the bottom ½" to ¾" of the stem before inserting. Any leaves left below the level of the mix would rot away, fostering a fungus condition that might spread to the stem itself.

Once you've inserted your cuttings in the pot or tray, mist daily until roots form. Mist only in the early morning, never at night. You can tell roots have formed if you tug gently on the cutting and it resists. However, don't try this until 2 weeks after making the cutting in the case of the sage, 3 weeks for rosemary, and at least 6 weeks for bay. Frequent, premature tug tests will disturb the cutting unnecessarily.

Once roots are established, remove the cuttings gently, shake off excess perlite and sand, and transplant them into 4" pots containing the regular soil/sand/peat moss/perlite planting mix. Soak thoroughly upon transplanting, place in a bright sunny window, and water thereafter whenever the plant mix looks dry to the eye, about every other day.

About 3 to 5 weeks after you transplant, when the young plants are around 3" to 4" high, pinch out the top center of each plant. This will make it bush out more effectively for a fuller, stronger plant. It will also give you another cutting if you want to start another plant. Be sure you get the stem and not just a leaf.

The hardy sage may be put out a month before the last spring frost date (that's April 15 in my garden), provided it's been acclimatized to outdoor weather. Wait until after the last spring frost date (May 15 in my garden) to put out the more tender bay and rosemary, also after acclimatizing.

Now to the third and probably most realistic way for most gardeners to get those three herbs started on their own. If you can't borrow cuttings from someone who has sage, rosemary, and bay plants indoors, then you'll simply have to wait until June and take cuttings from established plants in the gardens of friends or neighbors—who will not mind, because the herbs will be big and strong by then.

The procedure for taking, rooting, and transplanting cuttings is exactly the same as we just outlined. The new plants won't have quite as long a growing season as they would if you had been able to start them from cuttings off herbs indoors, but if you get them started in June, they'll still have plenty of time to develop.

A word of caution about bay: It is difficult, some would say almost impossible, to start bay plants from cuttings, and if you succeed, you deserve a medal. Part of the problem is that it takes 6 weeks for the bay cutting to develop roots, and if you allow the cuttings to get too dry, or too moist, for 2 or 3 days during that interval, the cutting may shrivel up or rot. With rosemary and sage cuttings, you can expect 95 to 98 percent success; with bay, no more than 50 percent.

That said, I encourage you to at least try growing bay in the way I have described. Don't take failure personally, because you're in the good company of professional growers. And remember, you can always buy a healthy bay plant for that first garden.

Take Your Choice: Herbs for All Seasons and Reasons

SOME OF THE HERBS INCLUDED in the herb garden plan are available in a number of different varieties, which I didn't mention earlier to avoid confusion. Actually, the range of your choice is governed by several constraints: in the case of the nine herbs we suggest starting from seed, by what's offered by your particular supplier of herb seed; in the case of the other six herbs to be propagated by division or cutting, by whatever varieties your friends or neighbors happen to have in their garden.

Anyway, let's look at the selection available among the basic cooking herbs. Sometimes there is only one standard variety. In other cases there are several to pick from. And in still others you have a veritable Baskin-Robbins panoply of choices. Part IV, the Herb Culture Guide, describes the most popular varieties of both culinary and nonculinary herbs, complete with information on propagation, care, and plant characteristics.

Chives

Allium schoenoprasum is the standard chive for kitchen use and the one that belongs in the basic culinary garden we've described. There's a fine-leafed version also, with about the same flavor, but it sometimes gets a little floppy in summer, so I don't recommend it.

Garlic chive is a productive plant with broad leaves and an attractive white flower. Years ago, many people didn't care for its garlic flavor, but now that garlic has become widely accepted in all kinds of cookery, this plant has grown in popularity and use.

Curly or curled chive, so named for its spiraling leaf, is pretty, but not nearly as productive and has maybe only 10 percent of the flavor of the standard chives. The same is true of the flowering varieties of chives planted from bulbs in the fall. There is also a giant allium, also started from bulbs, which reaches 3' to 4' in height. It produces very few useable chive leaves and is grown primarily for show.

Sweet Marjoram

This herb of the oregano family has such a strong flavor that it'll hit you even before you cut it or stir it up. It has thirty or so cousins, with various different growth patterns, but none with anything like sweet marjoram's distinctive flavor. That's why even a mediocre chef insists on the real thing, *Majorana hortensis*. The hardier wild marjoram simply doesn't have the coveted strong marjoram flavor.

Thyme

There are over 60 varieties of thyme, with distinct differences in appearances, growing patterns, and flavor.

The standard culinary thyme, *Thymus vulgaris* or common English thyme, grows in erect, shrublike fashion to about 12" to 15" in height. It is the best bet for new gardeners. French thyme, another variety of vulgaris, is shorter, with tiny, pointy leaves, and less hardy, but is held in high esteem, especially by French chefs.

Some thymes have un-thyme-like aromas. Caraway thyme smells like its fellow herb caraway, and orange balsam thyme and the lemon thymes have a powerful citrus fragrance.

Caraway thyme and wooly thyme—so named for its fuzzy leaf—grow in creeping fashion, low to the ground, rather than as erect small bushes. They are often planted in and around walkways because the plants release their pleasant odors to pedestrians when trod upon. Other creepers are labeled praecox or serphyllum and boast pink, white, red, or flesh-colored blossoms.

Certain thymes are grown mainly for their aesthetic value, usually as part praecox or of a collection of a wide variety of thymes in the garden. Some of these—golden lemon and silver lemon thyme, for example—have a lemony thyme flavor that adds piquancy to some dishes.

Basil

There are dozens of basils to pick from, divided into three basic groups.

Most Genovese basils, developed by growers in the Genoa, Italy, area, have the strong flavor sought in Italian recipes, including the multipurpose pesto sauce. Relatively new in the herb marketplace, Genovese varieties are being branded in the same way that certain other Italian exports—such as the cheese Parmigiano-Reggiano and the wine Chianti Classico—have been branded. What's in a name? One of the best Genovese varieties, in my opinion, is called Nufar, but its nondescript name has kept it from enjoying the popularity it deserves. Nufar is rich in flavor and aroma and tough enough to withstand Fusarium wilt, a disease that can wipe out an entire crop in a few days.

Small-leaved dwarf varieties of basil, such as the Minette and Spicy Globe varieties, are ideal for growing in small spaces and containers. Some cooks tell me these diminutive varieties with their smaller leaves and softer stems are much easier to chop and dice than their bigger brothers.

Large-leaved varieties, such as lettuce-leaf basil, take up a lot of room but are highly productive when they are pinched back at regular intervals; allowing them to flower will hinder their growth.

Other basils that will tempt the gardener-cook are the lemon-scented basils, many of which have been coming into the North American market from Asian growers in recent years, and also the purple-leaved varieties. Lemon basil is often used in fish dishes. Purple basil is a must for making basil vinegar, adding an attractive pink/lavender tint to the liquid. It is also an attractive garnish on salads and many other dishes.

Not all new basil varieties come from abroad. One of many friends I've made in the world of herbs is Dr. Jim Simon, a plant scientist at Purdue University for some years, and now at Rutgers. Jim has developed a basil with a delightful lemon fragrance, named Sweet Dani after his daughter, and a fragrant basil with dark green leaves and purple calyxes, named Magical Michael after his son.

Chervil

Chervil is another herb much favored by French chefs. It has a mild, sweet anise flavor and is easy to grow, even in partial shade. There are two basic varieties of chervil, one with a flat leaf, and one with a curled leaf. Flavor and plant size seem identical in both, so except for foliage aesthetics, it really doesn't matter which kind you choose for your herb garden.

Coriander/Cilantro

This relative of parsley was relatively unknown a few years ago, except in Indian and Mexican kitchens. It is now one of the most popular fresh herbs in the United States. It is grown for both the leaf, cilantro, and the seed, coriander. As the seed is readily available in any grocery store's spice department, we include it in the basic herb garden for its leaf production. Its leaves do resemble parsley leaves, but its overall growth pattern is similar to that of dill. It may be grown in rows, like dill or parsley, especially if you have big plans for using the foliage in salsa, soup, and other standard Tex-Mex fare.

An interesting stand-in for cilantro is Vietnamese coriander, which is not botanically related to coriander, but its leaves possess a strong cilantro flavor. As a cascading grower, it is suitable for planting in a hanging basket.

Parsley

Like chervil, here the basic choice is between the plain leaf and the curled leaf, only with parsley there's a wide variety within both groups. That's because the large garnish market for parsley in the restaurant trade has stimulated the development of new forms. Some seed companies offer five different varieties for the garnish trade, and each one claims to be curlier than the one before it. They're called Double Curled, Triple Curled, Multi-Curled, Optima, and Perfection.

I notice that chefs on the Food Network almost invariably stipulate flat leaf parsley and not the curly parsley for use in recipes. Italians definitely prefer it for cooking. In fact, that's why the flat leaf variety is often referred to as Italian parsley.

Mitsuba, a Japanese member of the parsley family, seems to be catching on these days as more people experiment with Asian cooking in their kitchens. It grows similarly to our parsley, but with stronger flavor and larger leaves, especially in its later stages of growth. It's easy to grow and is found in a number of seed catalogs.

Dill

There are three varieties of dill to choose from: common dill, dill bouquet, and fernleaf dill. Common dill grows bigger—to about 3' in my area—and produces more seed heads, but it may need staking, for if it grows too vigorously early in the season, its spindly form will be vulnerable to windy weather.

Dill bouquet is a bushier plant and does not produce seed heads in the profusion that common dill does. But if dill bouquet is planted at successive intervals in the season (as I recommend in the next chapter), it will serve your needs as well as the taller variety.

Fernleaf dill is a dwarf variety with attractive, lacy, dark green foliage. For a small plant it produces a large quantity of dill weed.

Summer Savory

There is only one summer savory, though it is sometimes confused with its relative, winter savory. Summer savory is the preferred variety for the basic garden. It's bigger and better tasting and easier to grow.

Winter savory tastes the same but is not as delicate in flavor. Its one advantage over summer savory is that it is a perennial. It grows in low bush form and can be trained for an attractive border or edging plant.

Mint

There are a couple of dozen mints, which vary in flavor and texture, in size of leaf, and in the height to which they grow.

By far the most popular mints are spearmint and peppermint. They have similar growth patterns and reach about the same height. Peppermint seems to have stronger stems, and it may well produce more foliage in the growing season, though frankly I've never counted. Peppermint comes in white-stemmed and black-stemmed varieties.

Spearmint is the better choice for food recipes—a deep, minty sauce for lamb, a flavoring in mint jelly, and a welcome addition to peas, carrots, and potatoes. The mint leaves also make a refreshing tea. Spearmint is known as "man's best excuse for drinking bourbon." Every spring during Kentucky Derby week, we sell hundreds of plants of our Kentucky spearmint variety for use in mint juleps.

The stronger flavor in peppermint makes it desirable for making candy, gum, and other sweets. Its leaves also may be used to brew delicious teas, hot or cold. Unlike spearmint, peppermint contains menthol, and that essential oil has been adapted in many ways for commercial and medicinal uses.

According to Jim Crosby, a mint farmer in Illinois, Wrigley's Doublemint chewing gum was traditionally made with equal portions of spearmint and peppermint. "Peppermint Jim" (as he is known) should know—his farm used to supply Wrigley with mint oil for its chewing gums and Colgate Palmolive with mint for its toothpastes.

Oregano

If you are interested in growing oregano with spicy, pizza-quality piquancy, there are several varieties worth your consideration.

Hot and Spicy oregano, a fairly recent introduction, is a compact but dense grower suitable for limited spaces and containers. Its rich, deep green leaves pack a fiery edge that will enliven any sauce.

Greek oregano is the spiciest of all the oreganos. Because it was developed from wild varieties growing in Greece, it has great diversity in leaf size, shape, color, and growth habit.

My favorite oregano is oregano Maru, a strongly flavored variety we have developed as Sal's Choice. It is the tallest of all the oreganos and one of the hardiest, yet it does not spread as much as other varieties, so is easier to control in the garden. And it packs the right kick.

So-called wild marjoram is often sold as "oregano" by seed companies who feel free to do so because in fact the Latin name for it is *Origanum vulgare*. This is not the true oregano, which still doesn't have a proper Latin name. Wild marjoram does not have the characteristics the good cook or the average Italian is looking for.

Though the botanical jury is still out on this one, it now appears that the true oregano is not related to marjoram as has long been believed. It is not an *Origanum* at all, but is in fact in the mint family.

Tarragon

French tarragon belongs to the *Artemisia* genus of herbs and is grown only from cuttings or divisions. It should not be confused with Russian tarragon, which can be grown from seed but lacks the fennel-anise flavor of true tarragon.

Sage

There are at least 500 varieties of this most prolific of the herbs, offering a multitude of subtle differences in flavor, color, and growing and flowering habits. Technically perennials, many of the sages are too tender to survive cold winters. That's why I recommend common gray sage to most newcomers. It's got good flavor, it's hardy, and it's available in numerous varieties. The dwarf variety of gray sage is a good choice for containers. Another compact grower of recent vintage is Berggarten sage. It produces rounded, very large silver-gray leaves that have a desirably strong sage flavor.

Sage is related to the popular garden flower salvia, and you'll see a fairly close resemblance between them in leaf configuration and overall growth pattern. Some sages, such as purple sage and tricolor sage, have a pleasing, decorative look, but generally they are weaker in flavor.

Rosemary

Rosemary grows in two distinctly different fashions. One variety is upright or bushlike, and the other creeps or cascades and so is more suited to hanging baskets or stone walls. Within the upright variety, there are four different types: one with blue flowers, one with white flowers, one with a bigger leaf than any of the others (Foresteri), and one with mixed flavor (Pine-Scented). With the exception of the last, all varieties, including the prostrate variety, yield the distinctive rosemary flavor so desirable in cooking.

A sharp rise in the demand for rosemary, both for its applications in cooking and for its essential oils, has led to the development of numerous new varieties. A very strong upright variety developed by growers in Israel is called Barbecue because its sturdy branches can be individually harvested and used as skewers on the grill. Sal's Choice is another new arrival from Israel. A vigorous grower with straight, upright stems and deep green foliage, it is one of the best rosemary varieties, and it boasts great flavor.

Bay

There's only one true culinary bay—*Laurus nobilis*. It is a full-fledged tree in its native tropical climate—growing to thirty feet in a lifetime—but in most parts of this country we know it as a mere sprig, and so value it more. A bay specimen plant of 2' or 3' in height in our area may take 8 years to grow and will have a retail value of $100. A California variety of bay features a longer, narrower leaf and a eucalyptus-like flavor, not desirable for cooking.

Maintaining the First Garden

THERE ARE A NUMBER OF TRICKS, techniques, or procedures that can help you keep your first garden healthy and productive throughout the actual growing season. Let's look at them now.

Cultivate Ten Minutes a Week

A certain amount of weeding, by hand or with a small three- or four-prong hand cultivator, is required in any garden once it has been planted, though herbs pose nothing like the chore of keeping a good-sized vegetable patch clean.

It's especially important to keep the garden free of weeds early in the season. Except the mints, most herbs are slow growers and won't be able to compete with weeds unless you help. For a 65- to 75-square-foot garden, if you devote a mere 10 minutes once a week to the weeds, you should fully master them by July. The only new ones to appear after that will be random weeds that sprout from seed carried into the garden by the wind or birds, not from weed seed in the original soil mix. By that time, the herbs themselves will be fully developed and in no danger from the intruders.

Don't Mulch in Season

Spreading mulch material in the herb garden in an effort to suppress weeds is a bad idea because it tends to keep the soil too moist, which is just what you don't want, and also promotes fungus. An herb garden is small enough to keep weed-free by hand, no matter how busy you are with other things. As my father used to say, "To keep a good garden, all you need is a sharp hoe and a strong back."

Irrigate Sparingly

The herbalist Adelma Simmons used to grow a variety of plants at Caprilands Herb Farm in Coventry, Connecticut. Then one summer we had a terrible drought in the Northeast. Adelma discovered that the only plants that withstood the drought were the herbs, and thereafter she limited her plantings to herbs.

Herbs like it dry, so wait longer than you might be inclined to before watering an established herb garden. There will be times in July or August, especially in a particularly dry summer, when you definitely should provide water, but if you're at all in doubt about it, test the soil first. Simply drive a spade or trowel into any bare area. If the soil is bone dry to a depth of 6", drag out the hose or watering can. Keep foliage dry by watering gently but thoroughly at the base of the plants.

Flowers and vegetables need watering about three times as often as herbs do. There is no such thing as a "typical" summer, I suppose, but if there were, you might have to water your vegetable garden five or six times in the course of it, and your herb garden only twice.

Side Dress Basil, Coriander, Parsley, and Dill

These are the only four herbs in the basic garden that require a bit of extra fertilization in season to maximize their output. If you use a liquid fertilizer like fish emulsion or liquid seaweed, feed these herbs every 2 to 3 weeks after setting them out, or after sprouting. If you use dried cow manure or good compost, scratch it into the soil around the plantings twice: once when the plants are 4" to 6" high, and again in mid-July.

Do not fertilize the other herbs in the garden or you will promote excessive leafy growth. This will diminish the manufacture of essential oils from which most herbs get their distinctive aromas and flavors. The flavor does not develop proportionately in overstimulated leaf growth.

Other herbs that would also require a side dressing in season are the so-called salad herbs—sorrel, roquette, cress, mustard, and corn salad. These herbs, which are cut primarily for their leaves, benefit from fertilization in increased leaf production.

Pinch Out Basil

The best way to get very bushy and productive basil plants is to pinch out the top of the center stem on each plant about the time the plants are 6" to 8" tall. This will prevent the plant from growing straight up, going into its flowering stage, and getting floppy, and will promote fuller growth in the lower branches. You have to pinch out only that initial time if you use basil regularly, because during the rest of the season, every time you harvest the basil you'll be pinching it back at the same time. If you don't let basil go into flower, it will be more productive for you. At the same time, the basil will be less likely to attractive Japanese beetles, if that persistent challenge to gardeners happens to be present in your area.

Sow Succession Crops of Dill and Coriander

To have fresh dill and coriander on hand throughout the harvest season, make four to five sowings of their seed, or one sowing every 3 weeks up until 10 weeks before the fall frost date. I make my last sowing of dill on August 1 in order to harvest ripened seed prior to October 10, the average date of the first fall frost in our area. If you use just the foliage—the dill weed or the coriander—keep sowing seed up to September 1.

Succession sowing of dill is especially important if you're growing cucumbers for preserving and want to use your own fresh dill in the preserving process. You can't always predict when you'll be doing your pickling, so it's better to have the seed on hand throughout. Don't forget, dill leaves add the right flavor to your pickling brew, too. Seeds are favored because they look so good inside the Mason jars.

Use a sawed-off cardboard carton as a frame for making various sowings, following the outdoor sowing techniques described earlier for Group 3 herbs.

Bug Problems

Insects *will* show up in an herb garden. True, most herbs are not attractive to bugs, and many herbs even repel them. But if insects do appear, as will happen in some seasons with more frequency than in others, it is important to be on the alert for them every time you go out to the garden to cultivate or harvest.

First, what not to do. Because all parts of most of the herbs in the culinary garden are destined for human consumption, I strongly recommend that you not use any form of chemical insecticide or pesticide when bugs appear. I'd avoid using the so-called organic rotenone and pyrethrin products, too. Poison is poison, whether it's made in the field or the factory.

To cope with the larger forms of insects—such as the voracious caterpillars that prey on parsley, dill, and fennel and will strip these plants bare if you let them—simply handpick the invader and dispose of it outside the garden.

To deal with smaller insects, such as white fly, spider mite, and aphid, mix a batch of Nana's Bug Juice (see page 47) and spray the invaders with that. Include a few fresh leaves of basil in the batch for added potency. Don't forget to spray *under* the leaves. If you don't want to make your own mixture, look for one of the commercial versions of our homemade repellent now available in garden centers.

Some gardeners swear by the technique of dispersing beneficial insects, such as ladybugs, into the garden as mercenary soldiers to combat aphids and other insects. Other gardeners reject this approach on the grounds that the hired hands might well move to somebody else's garden the moment they are set out. In any case, the beneficials are available through many seed and plant catalogs.

Don't just turn your garden hose on pests to spray them off the plant, as some people have advised. Psychologically it may give you a boost to see harmful insects temporarily in rout. The problem is, the powerful stream of water from the hose will knock your plants for a loop. You won't kill them, but the battering will surely set them back.

Harvesting and Storing Herbs

MANY FIRST-TIME HERB GARDENERS don't realize how quickly they can start harvesting from their new plants. Within a few weeks of planting you can begin to snip from the herbs, and for the sake of productivity, you should. The more regularly you harvest throughout the summer, the more new growth you will stimulate.

Harvest with a sharp knife or pruning shears, and don't cut into any hard woody growth. If you cut 2" to 3" down from the tips of branches, you'll get the youngest and most flavorsome cuttings.

If and when the herbs get ahead of you—and such fast growers as oregano, chives, and basil might do that—cut them in quantity for freezing or for hanging to dry. The plants will put forth new growth in short order.

Most annual herbs can be harvested in quantity—cut to within 4" to 6" of ground level—at least three or four times in a season, and more often if your growing season is particularly long. In taking early harvests of the annuals, don't chop them down to ground level or the plants won't recover sufficiently to give you later harvests. Chives and parsley are the exceptions; they can recover from severe pruning.

Established perennials in their second or subsequent seasons can be harvested a number of times, too. Don't cut them too fully too late in the season, though, or they may become too weak to get through winter. Generally, never cut into the woody growth of any perennial unless you're deliberately trying to limit its growth.

The annuals and tender perennials in the herb garden should be cut prior to the first expected frost in the fall. If there's any doubt about the weather, cut the herbs down anyway, as they won't grow much more thereafter even if you could get away with leaving them in for another few weeks. In the first garden, that means harvesting all the basil, chervil, coriander, and dill.

Continue to cut as needed from the hardy perennials and the biennial parsley beyond the first frost and throughout the fall. The flavor of some herbs—sage in particular—is improved by a couple of frosts, so don't turn your back on the garden just because the nights become cold. Not until you get a deep freeze, which in our area may not come until Thanksgiving, will the productive cycle of the plants come to a close for the year.

Saving Herbs for Winter

Culinary herbs can be saved for winter use in cold climates by drying, freezing, or storing in vinegar. No single method is best for all herbs. And there is no single assembly-line process for each method of preserving that works for all herbs, or for all kitchens, either. Some special harvesting and storing tips are noted for the individual culinary herbs in the Sources, page 238. Here are general guidelines:

The best time to harvest most of the basic cooking herbs for saving—whether in dried form, frozen form, or vinegars—is just before the plant flowers, because that's when oil content is highest. Two obvious exceptions are true French tarragon, which does not go into flower under any circumstances, and bay, which produces seed only in its balmy native climate. Another exception might be sweet marjoram, simply because many cooks like to take it in full flower and preserve the tiny blossoms along with the foliage. Also, if dill and coriander are being grown for their seed, then they must be taken long after the flowering process has begun, when the seed heads start to ripen.

The best time of day to harvest for saving is mid-morning on a sunny day, after the dew has burned off and when the plants are at peak flavor.

Some herbs may need to be washed clean of dirt before processing, especially low and sprawling growers, such as the marjoram, oregano, and thyme.

I know people who are so particular about their herbs that they will shake them clean rather than put them in water. If your herbs do need a rinse, use cold water, for hot water definitely does draw out the oils prematurely.

Drying is the best way to preserve most of the herbs, if the right conditions can be provided. An old-fashioned attic or an unused closet is ideal for drying herbs if it is warm, dark, dry, and well ventilated.

- Herbs need warmth because that way they dry more quickly, and the faster they dry (up to a point), the better the aromatic oils are retained.
- They need darkness because the absence of light keeps the herbs from losing their distinctive colors and flavors.
- They must be dry and well ventilated because both these conditions hasten the drying process and also discourage mold.

So, whether or not you have an old-fashioned attic or dark, dry spare closet or room, these are the conditions to strive for.

The herbs can be hung in small bunches to dry, or arranged in thin layers on clean paper cookie sheets or paper towels or—preferably—on screens of some mesh material to permit better air flow. When collecting the dried seed is the object—as with dill and coriander—paper bags can be used to enclose the bunches.

My preferred way to dry herbs is to lay out paper towels, spread the herbs on them, and cover with more paper towels and a layer of newspaper. Herbs dried in this manner may take from 2 days to 2 weeks to become fully dry, depending on the individual herb and the actual conditions that exist. Most herbs processed in this manner will dry nicely within a week's time.

Herbs can be dried more quickly in a kitchen oven, but care must be taken not to apply too much heat, or the aromatic oils will evaporate and some of the herbs will darken considerably.

The average human body temperature of 98.6°F is just about the perfect heat for curing most herbs. If your oven lacks a setting below 200°F it may be hard to get the heat low enough even if you leave the oven door ajar.

It's relatively easy to cure herbs, as well as fruits and vegetables, in home food dehydrators, and these devices offer great precision. Microwave ovens have also been used for this purpose. Each manufacturer has its own guidelines, so you may have to experiment with this method. Generally, microwaving 10 sprigs of any herb will yield about 1 to 2 tablespoons of the finished product.

Once dried, herbs must be stored properly or they'll lose their potency. Put them in air-tight glass jars with screw-type lids and keep in a dark place away from the excessive heat. If you can't store them in a cupboard or some other dark spot, use opaque or colored glass jars.

After drying and storing the herbs, keep checking the jars for several days to be sure no moisture appears on the inside of the glass. If this happens, it means the herbs aren't fully dry yet, and mold or fermentation will occur unless you remove them and finish the drying.

Two important additional points about dried herbs for use in cooking:

+ In dried form herbs are usually three or four times more powerful than in fresh form. When recipes call for a certain amount of the fresh herb, and you are using the dried herb, cut your portion by a third.

+ Most dried herbs do not retain their aroma longer than a year, even under ideal storage conditions. Dried herbs should be checked for flavor every fall and renewed from the current garden.

With some herbs, freezing works as well as, and in certain cases better than drying does. Some cooks claim that freezing basil, chives, and parsley, in particular, is preferable to drying.

To use this technique, first wash the herbs in cold water, then let dry. Freeze the sprigs and leaves in small amounts in plastic bags. After freezing, simply use each portion as needed, dropping it into your dish frozen rather than letting it thaw.

Vinegar is another convenient and almost foolproof medium for preserving the flavor of fresh herbs—especially dill, basil, rosemary, and tarragon—into the winter months. Most good cookbooks have plenty of simple vinegar recipes to choose from.

Freeze-drying herbs is a relatively new technique, effective although expensive, and it retains the herbs' original colors and aromas.

Even if you don't think you have the right attic or drying room, or the right jars, or you can't afford any of the latest labor-saving devices on the market, try drying some of your own herbs. Experiment and improvise with what you do have: you will have success, and you'll become much more adept at dealing with next year's harvest in the bargain.

Steps to Take for the Second Spring

AN HERB GARDEN is far from finished when the first season is over, and that's the beauty of it.

It can be brought indoors if a number of simple but carefully planned steps are taken, as we'll explain in the next chapter.

And it can be renewed with little effort in the following year—indeed, the perennial herbs will renew themselves, without your assistance, if they are left to develop on their own.

Let's look at the schedule of activities for the second and subsequent years before considering the more complex undertaking of bringing live herb plants indoors.

Mulch Perennials after a Deep Freeze

The herb garden should be mulched at the end of the growing season to protect all the perennials, some of which are more tender than others, from a severe winter.

Mulching will also keep the herbs from coming alive prematurely during a midwinter warm spell—the January thaw that many cold-winter regions sometimes get.

Mulching is especially important if there has been a series of consecutive mild winters. Then the herbs will be acclimatized to those conditions and even more vulnerable when the hard winter comes.

The time to mulch is when the ground is frozen solid to a depth of one inch. It takes three consecutive nights in the low 20s to do it. When this happens, mulch the entire garden with a 6" layer of salt hay—if you can obtain that superior natural insulator—or leaves, and lay some small branches or narrow boards down on top to keep the material in place. Natural seed-free mulch materials, such as Mainely Mulch, are now available in garden centers and nurseries for spreading on garden beds.

Clean Up the Garden

After all danger of a lasting snowfall is past (by the end of March in my area), remove the mulch from the herb garden. (Leaving the mulch on too long could create a problem by heating the garden up prematurely. Some of the plants will start growing rapidly; then, when you finally remove the mulch, the new growth may have rotted for lack of light and air circulation.)

Trim off all the old growth on the perennials from which you want new shoots—namely the mint, marjoram, oregano, and tarragon. The old growth, besides looking bad, gets in the way of new growth and encourages fungus and disease. Sage and thyme plants won't need trimming, except for dead growth, because they don't die back to the ground like the others.

Move and Divide

If you want to move any of the perennials to different locations, early spring is the time to do it, while the root systems are supporting relatively little growth. Maybe you put in too much of one herb last year and want to cut it back. Maybe you want to improve the aesthetic or practical arrangement in the garden or just dig and divide for the sake of doing it. Depending on your tastes, you may now want to expand a planting of one type of herb, or make some substitutions for the herbs you found you didn't use that much last year.

With the exception of mint, none of the perennials in your first garden are likely to have overreached themselves on their own by this time. In subsequent years they will, though, and this early spring period is the ideal time to tackle them.

Loosen and Replenish the Soil

Loosen the soil in the garden areas where this year's crop of annuals will go. Mix some good compost, rabbit manure, or dehydrated sheep or cow manure into the soil as you go. Dried chicken and even turkey manure are now available as commercial products. Transplant your new annuals to these spots after all danger of frost is past.

You may notice some volunteer seedlings of dill or maybe even savory. This will happen if the annuals from last year's garden were allowed to go to seed. Somehow some of the seeds have survived the winter and produced new plants for you. Unless they're in the way, let them be, or move them to a more desirable location.

Sow Annuals Indoors

Beginning in February and March (where the last spring frost date is in May), sow seed for all annuals and other new plants indoors. Locate new and/or better sources of seeds, divisions, and cuttings.

After the Second Year

The perennial growth in the second year will not be so great as to warrant major attention, but by the third spring, you'll need to take some action to avoid possible overcrowded conditions. Plants will not always grow so vigorously as to interfere with the overall garden plan by the third season, but often they will. One year I built a culinary garden for one of my customers that featured a small tarragon plant in the center. The next time I stopped by was 2 years later, by which time a very happy tarragon plant had grown 4' across and virtually taken over the whole garden.

Bear in mind that perennials by definition add to their growth every year. The very first customer I waited on as a kid was looking for a mature sage plant for her herb garden. My father directed me to one that was 6 years old. Its roots were so extensive it took me a half hour to dig it out. Right from the start I knew gardening was a physically demanding business.

Bringing Herb Plants Indoors

YOU CAN GROW ALL FIFTEEN culinary herbs indoors over the winter—though with greatly reduced productivity—if you can give them the right conditions.

But you can't just dig up all the plants from your existing garden outdoors and expect them to survive among your lampshades and bookshelves.

Developing new young, strong plants is really the key to having a small but vigorous herb garden inside the house over the winter months.

Also, you must have the right spot to put the herbs in their pots. If you can keep the herbs on a shelf or tray or indoor box with a full southern exposure, then the new plants will repay the effort it took you to get them started.

Starting from Seed

Most herb plants for indoor locations should be started fresh from seeds a month or so before your fall frost date—Labor Day weekend is when we get our clay pots and seed packets out again.

Among these are all the annuals:

basil

chervil

coriander

dill

summer savory

There's no sense in trying to bring any of these indoors as potted plants directly from your garden—even though you see them flourishing out there about this time—because as annuals they will become leggy and quickly expire behind closed doors.

I also recommend starting fresh from seed for these perennials:

sage

thyme

marjoram

chives

and the biennial:

parsley

Sage can be started from a cutting, but it's much easier to get it going from seed this time of year.

Thyme and marjoram can be started from division, but it is not always convenient to do so, either because the garden plan calls for the existing plants to spread more, or because the plants as they mature simply become too hard to divide and replant into a small pot.

Chives and parsley could be dug up and brought indoors in pots, but the pots would have to be at least 6" wide to accommodate their bigger root systems.

Anyway, all ten of these herbs can be started from seed using the sowing techniques described earlier.

About 5 to 6 weeks before the first frost, fill 4" clay pots with the proper mix of soil, peat, and perlite, then bury the pots up to their necks in the garden.

Cluster sow seed for each of the herbs in these individual pots, cover with fine sand, and let germinate. Fertilize with fish emulsion or liquid seaweed when the sprouts are 3" to 4" high. Before the first frost they'll all be ready to come indoors as fresh herbs, with lots of moderate growing ahead of them.

Starting from Division

Three of the remaining five herbs should be started from division just before frost time. These are:

mint

oregano

tarragon

After you've harvested the tops of these herbs in the fall, divide them according to the techniques described earlier for Group 4 plants, then put the divisions into 6" pots and bury the pots in the ground for three good freezes. (The 4" pots are too small for containing root divisions.) This will give them time to recoup their energies and will prevent premature growth indoors, which would weaken them. When you're ready to mulch the garden, dig out the three pots and bring them in.

There are some mints that don't take to this technique. Spearmint, curly mint, and golden mint all have the habit of losing their leaves once brought indoors, and they won't revive until February. Peppermint, pineapple mint, orange mint, bergamot mint, and pennyroyal, among others, will come indoors without going into a coma.

French tarragon also starts to lose its leaves and appears to be a lost cause in December, but like the spearmint it will put forth new growth again in early February, especially if you remember it in your prayers.

Importing from the Garden

Bay and rosemary are the only herbs in our basic culinary garden that can be brought into the house for the winter as is. If you planted these in clay pots originally as suggested, all you have to do is dig them up just before the first heavy frost. If not in pots, take care in digging them up, especially the bay, which will have put down a large tap root.

If you've used 6" clay pots for all these procedures, you can fit all fifteen herbs into a tray or frame that measures 4' long by 12" wide by 3" to 4" deep. Clay pots are superior to plastic pots for indoor use because they are porous and the plants won't get waterlogged in them so easily.

With such a tray, you can construct a kind of window box for the inside of a picture window with southern exposure, and have a perfect place for locating the herb garden. You can make the box out of wood and stain it or paint it to match your woodwork. More important for the herbs, you should install a leak-proof metal, plastic, or aluminum-foil tray inside the box. Line this with pebbles to a depth of 2" and place your potted herbs on top of it. This will ensure that, when you do water the herbs, excess moisture will drain from the pots.

Herb plants indoors in winter should be lightly fertilized with fish emulsion or liquid seaweed every 2 weeks to keep them growing well. The plants are confined in pots. They can't spread their roots out in search of food, so the food has to come to them.

Irrigate herbs when the soil feels dry to the touch, but don't drown them. Overwatered herbs rot quickly.

You may have bug problems indoors, especially if you also have a profusion of houseplants. Nana's Bug Juice (see page 47) works indoors as well as outdoors, so use it to control insect problems. Stay away from poisonous sprays when dealing with the edible herbs. I don't recommend washing the plants with soap and water solutions, either, as a lot of people do. It spoils the taste of plants that you're growing for the taste in the first place.

III.

Herb Garden
Plans

How to Use the Plans

THE GARDEN PLANS PRESENTED in this section may be followed precisely to create your own herb garden with good results, but they are offered here mainly as examples of the rich and diverse possibilities in herb gardening. Your personal tastes and needs, as well as the special qualities and limitations of the space in which you are toiling, will determine the type of garden, or combination of gardens herein, most suitable for you. I have adopted the 8' x 8' size (64 square feet) purely for convenience and ease of reference in comparing the space needs and growing habits of different herbs.

A brief introduction to each plan points out any factors particular to successfully growing the garden in question. For example, the Allium Garden needs a well-limed, fertilized soil for the best production. But unless otherwise noted, the general methods and conditions presented in the main text apply to all the gardens.

The herbs in each plan are listed alphabetically by popular name, along with information on their particular **life cycle, average height,** and suggested **propagation method.**

More detailed cultural information specific to each herb mentioned in this book, including the botanical (Latin) name, is in the Herb Culture Guide, beginning on page 183.

Generally, most herbs will thrive in the growing conditions discussed in the main text. In some cases, though, additional steps are necessary to make sure an individual herb does well; I note this in the Herb Culture Guide where applicable. For example, several of the large-growing herbs, such as borage and lemon verbena, require a richer soil than most other herbs to do well, so we suggest composting or manuring the sections of the herb gardens where these herbs will be planted. Most perennial herbs with strong growing patterns need regular subdivision to confine them to a specific growing area. Some herbs, such as woad and St. John's wort, are prone to prolific self-sowing and may become a nuisance in the garden. These various characteristics are noted in the Herb Culture Guide where they apply, along with steps you can take to prevent the problems.

With each plan, the **life cycle** of each herb included is given in a simple abbreviated form as follows:

A	annual
B	biennial
P	perennial
TP	tender perennial

The **average height** is necessarily somewhat nebulous. It means how tall a mature plant will be on about Labor Day in a typical growing season, assuming you don't live in the southern parts of Florida, Texas, or California, where much greater growth will sometimes occur. If the plant is a perennial, the figure also presupposes that the plant has been properly trimmed and/or subdivided from time to time to fit its garden space.

The **propagation method** suggested for each herb in the plans is listed as a number, indicating one of the five methods discussed in the main text:

Group 1	Cluster sowing indoors
Group 2	Spot sowing indoors
Group 3	Cluster or row sowing outdoors
Group 4	Root division
Group 5	Stem cutting

The **bulb method** of propagation is included for certain plants, mostly alliums.

For the most part, these are realistic recommendations. In some cases, the horticulture method suggested may not be the easiest, but for most gardeners it will be the most convenient. For example, we frequently suggest starting an herb from seed, by either Group 1, 2, or 3 method, even though it might be easier to propagate the herb via cutting or division, because in these cases a mature version of the plant under discussion may be hard to locate.

An asterisk (*) appears next to the names of the fifteen basic culinary herbs whenever they are used in the plans.

You'll notice one more code: those herbs that are natural houseplant material have their **life cycle** abbreviations enclosed in brackets, such as [A], [P], or [TP]. This designation generally refers to smaller plants with relatively simple root systems, which can be contained in reasonably small pots, and which will prosper in a sunny window during the winter months. However, the code also covers such herbs as bay, eucalyptus, lemon verbena, orange osage, and rosemary, which can be successfully brought indoors in large pots, even as 6-footers. In some plans, pathways have been included; these may be made of gravel, stepping stones, or other suitable materials available to the gardener.

Culinary Garden: Year One

THE FIFTEEN BASIC cooking herbs have been arranged in practical and aesthetically pleasing patterns.

The tarragon plant is in the middle because it grows faster than the other perennials and so should make the best focal point.

The other perennials are placed symmetrically around the borders, where they'll be easy to get out. More important, they'll have enough room to develop in the second year.

The two mints are surrounded by boards (or some similar barrier) sunk to a depth of 12" to 16", which should keep their fast-growing root systems contained.

The annual herbs (with the exception of the chervil) are set in an inner circle around the tarragon. Flat stepping stones have been placed in the garden to provide easy access to the annuals in the middle.

At season's end, the bay and rosemary must be brought inside in pots, as they will not survive the winter outside, at least not in northern regions. The chives should be cut back at season's end. Harvest all annuals one last time just before the first frost. Pull up their root systems and remove them to keep the garden clean.

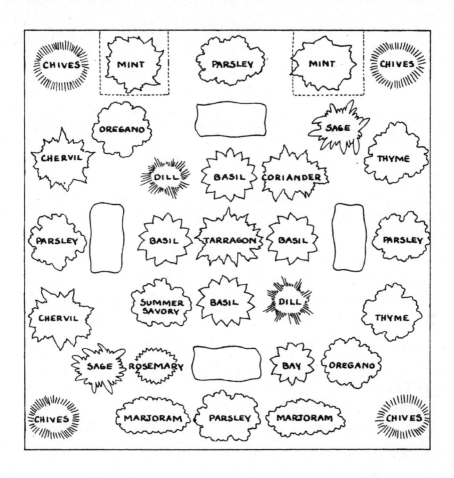

Culinary Garden: Year Two

TO RESTORE THE GARDEN POPULATION for the new growing season, resow or replant all the annuals, and bring out the rosemary and bay from indoors. Transplant these last two into slightly larger pots, then bury the pots in the garden.

The biennial parsley will grow rapidly early in the second season. Harvest it promptly, as it will go to seed quickly. Then dig up all existing parsley plants and sow new parsley for a fresh crop to replace the first year's crop. The deep tap roots on the parsley plants require digging out with a spade, rather than simply uprooting by hand. By this time the new parsley will be coming along.

Watch for unwanted volunteers appearing early in spring in the spots where last year's dill, coriander, and chervil grew, and also around oregano and marjoram, the two perennials with a knack for dropping seed. Self-sowing will occur more often in a garden that was not assiduously harvested or one that was well mulched for winter—the mulch protects the fallen seed through the cold.

This particular garden doesn't depend on the herbs to self-sow, but if it happens, and you have room to accommodate the seedlings where they are, or even elsewhere (though remember, these annuals do not always transplant well), by all means keep them.

Replace any perennial herbs that suffered damage over the winter months or have not grown to your expectations for one reason or another.

At the end of the second season: Bring the bay and rosemary back indoors in their pots. If they have put on a lot of growth during the season, transplant them into larger pots—but not too much larger. Generally, don't increase pot diameter by more than 2" or 3" in a season.

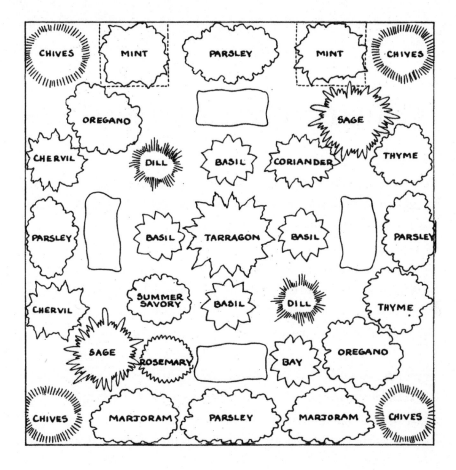

Dig up the tarragon, divide, and relocate where the bay grew.

Divide the chives and mints, if they're getting too big.

Confine the root systems of the oregano and marjoram by trimming with a sharp edging tool, removing the unwanted peripheral roots, and refilling those areas with fresh compost or soil.

Clip the branches of the sage if that plant has gotten too big for its assigned place.

Do the same for the thyme. If it has flopped over and taken root around its borders, spade out the unwanted portions. Any excess can be used as filler in a rock garden or patio area, or any other appropriate spot in your yard.

Culinary Garden: Year Three

NOW THE CYCLE of tasks becomes more familiar as they begin to repeat.

Bring the rosemary back outdoors, this time to center stage in the garden. It should be nearly 2' high and 12" to 14" wide.

Bring the bay back outdoors.

Replant annuals.

Keep the established parsley cut back; sow fresh parsley as in preceding year.

If any end-of-second-year tasks described earlier were not completed, do them now at the beginning of the third year:

+ Dig up and replant in smaller forms the chives, mints, and tarragon. By this time, they surely will have spread too wide for the limited space available to them in this garden.
+ Replace your thyme, as older woody plants will not be as productive.
+ By the end of this third year in the garden, you will know the needs of your plants and your own needs well enough to handle things smoothly and at precisely the right time.

HERB	LIFE CYCLE	AVERAGE HEIGHT	PROPAGATION METHOD
*basil	A	18"	2
*bay	[TP]	2' to 6'	5
*chervil	A	24"	2
*chives	P	12"	1
*coriander	A	24"	2
*dill	A	30"	3

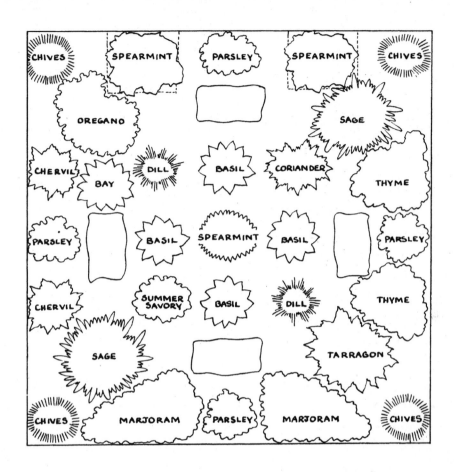

HERB	LIFE CYCLE	AVERAGE HEIGHT	PROPAGATION METHOD
*marjoram	TP	12"	1
*oregano	P	12" to 24"	4
*parsley	B	8"	3
*rosemary	[TP]	12" to 24"	3
*sage	P	24"	5
*summer savory	A	18" to 24"	3
*spearmint	P	18"	4
*tarragon	P	18" to 24"	4
*thyme	P	12"	1

Trattoria Garden

THIS GARDEN INCLUDES lots of the basil and parsley varieties popular in Italy and an ample supply of that mainstay of Italian cuisine, garlic. Rosemary plants are in 14" clay pots buried to a depth leaving 4" of rim above the soil. The cloves for the 50 garlic plants should be planted in the fall to ensure an early harvest date the following summer. Successive sowing of the arugula, or roquette—for example, April 15, June 15, and September 1 (in gardens in the Northeast), will ensure a season-long supply of this piquant salad ingredient.

HERB	LIFE CYCLE	AVERAGE HEIGHT	PROPAGATION METHOD
arugula	A	10"	3
Genovese basil	A	12" to 30"	2
garlic	P	24"	bulb
oregano Hot and Spicy	P	8"	4
parsley Comune	B	18"	3
*rosemary	[TP]	12" to 24"	5
*sage	P	24"	3
oregano thyme	P	8"	5

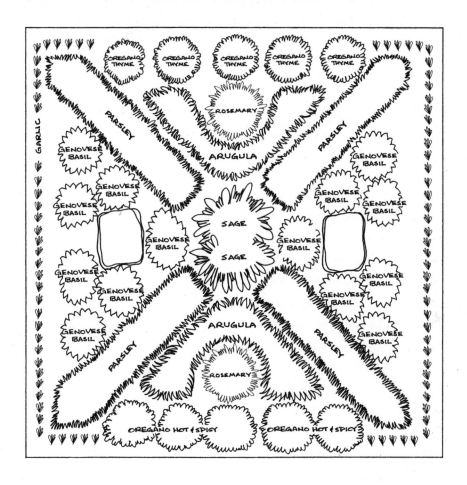

Taste of Asia Garden

(3' x 12')

THIS GARDEN DEPLOYS the distinctively flavored herbs used in Asian cuisine and made popular in recent years in non-Asian households due to the proliferation of Thai and Vietnamese restaurants in many of our cities. The garden happens to be very pleasing to the eye, too. The dark green mitsuba, sometimes called Japanese parsley, contrasts with the pale green, lacelike foliage of the neighboring saltwort. Likewise, the pale green lemon basil is a striking companion to the Thai basil with its leaves tinged with purple. The large perillas add their own splashes of purple to this layout.

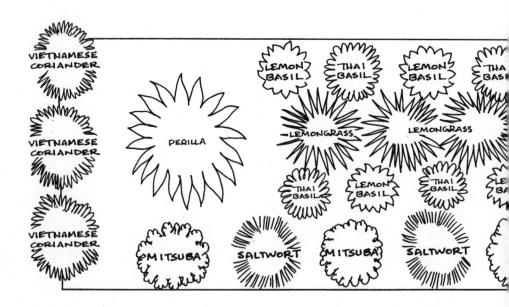

HERB	LIFE CYCLE	AVERAGE HEIGHT	PROPAGATION METHOD
lemon basil	A	15"	2
Thai basil	A	18" to 24"	2
Vietnamese coriander	A	4"	5
lemongrass	TP	36"	2
mitsuba	P	8" to 10"	2
perilla (shiso)	A	18" to 30"	3
saltwort	A	8" to 12"	1

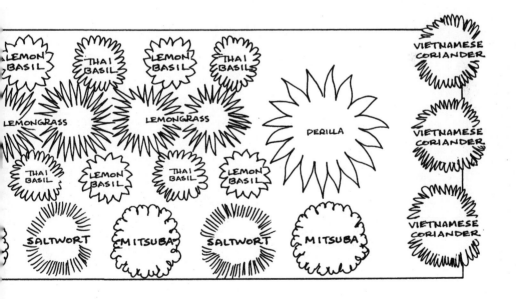

Tex-Mex Garden

(4' x 12')

THE CORIANDER, NOW KNOWN more popularly as cilantro, is given lots of room in this garden and should be sown at 4- to 6-week intervals for maximum productivity. Lime basil and cayenne pepper accentuate flavors popular in Mexican cooking. Epazote is utilized in many bean dishes, while the strongly flavored black peppermint anchors recipes for soups and stews.

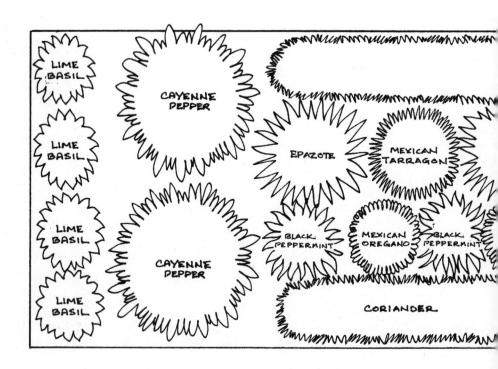

HERB	LIFE CYCLE	AVERAGE HEIGHT	PROPAGATION METHOD
lime basil	A	16" to 24"	2
cayenne pepper	A	30"	2
*coriander	A	24"	2
epazote	A	24" to 30"	3
Mexican oregano	TP	24" to 30"	5
black peppermint	P	18"	4
Mexican tarragon	P	14" to 18"	2/5

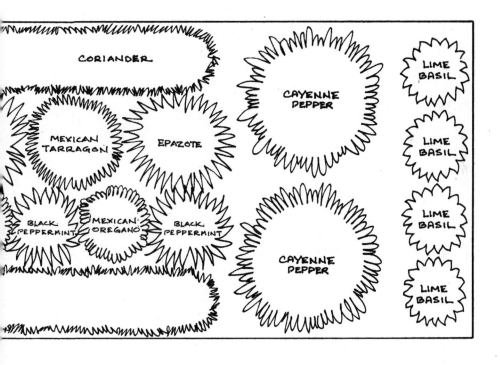

French Chef Garden

(4' x 16')

THIS GARDEN IS MORE SPACIOUS than some others because French chefs seem to make use of herbs in their recipes more than most cooks. Sweet marjoram, French thyme, French tarragon, and chervil are in constant play in the French kitchen. The celery-like flavor of lovage is put to use in many poultry and vegetable recipes. Lavender is sometimes used in place of thyme or tarragon; its flowers are incorporated in some French pastries. This plan calls for the bay and rosemary to be buried in 14" pots with the rims of the pots exposed about 4" above the soil. The rows of garlic should be planted in the fall; shallots and leeks go in during early spring. Resow the chervil and dill at intervals in the growing season for maximum production.

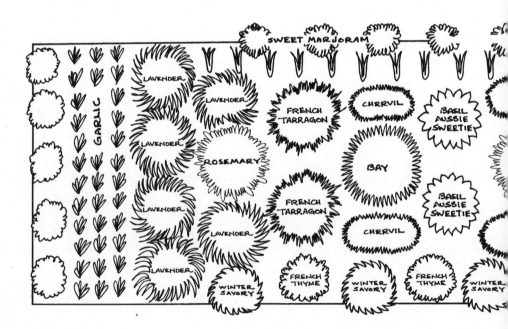

HERB	LIFE CYCLE	AVERAGE HEIGHT	PROPAGATION METHOD
basil Aussie Sweetie	A	36"	5
*bay	[TP]	2' to 6'	5
*chervil	A	12"	2
fernleaf dill	A	15"	3
garlic	P	24"	bulb
lavender	P	18"	2/5
leeks	P	24"	1
lovage	P	6'	2
*sweet marjoram	TP	12"	1
*rosemary	[TP]	12" to 24"	5
winter savory	P	8"	2
shallots	P	12"	bulb
French tarragon	P	18" to 24"	4
French thyme	P	12"	1

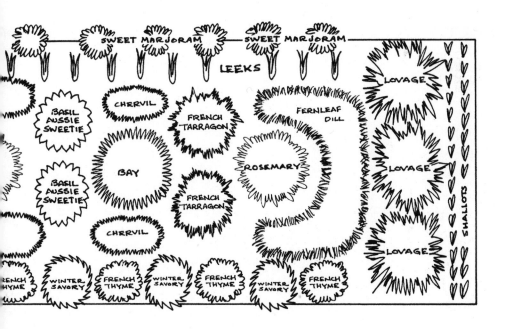

French Chef Garden

Annual Garden

THIS PLAN IS OFFERED mainly to show the most popular annual varieties at a glance. However, it could be used by people who are not able to garden in the same location for more than 1 year. The nasturtium and the versatile basil have been planted in quantity because they make attractive rows. The borage provides a good centerpiece because of its upright growth and pretty blue flowers. The entire garden could be planted in one day—with the exception of basil, if there is still a chance of cold nights.

HERB	LIFE CYCLE	AVERAGE HEIGHT	PROPAGATION METHOD
anise	A	24"	3
*basil	A	18"	2
purple basil	A	18"	2
borage	A	30"	2
chamomile	A	18" to 24"	2
chervil	A	12"	2
garden cress	A	6"	3
*dill	A	30"	3
fennel	A	30"	3
rose geranium	A	24"	5
mustard	A	18"	3
nasturtium	A	8"	3
roquette	A	10"	3
*summer savory	A	18" to 24"	3

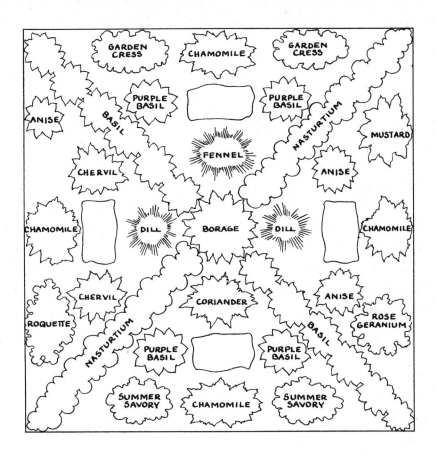

Perennial Garden

HERE'S A PLAN for people who don't want to fuss with annuals every year. By the end of the first season, the majority of the herbs here will have established a full and vigorous growth pattern. During the second year, the bay, rosemary, thyme, and winter savory will have done the same. Early in the second year, watch the sorrel carefully because it tends to get big and floppy and go to seed quickly, which makes leaves tough and bitter. If you trim it continuously early in the second year, it will keep its place and its good flavor.

HERB	LIFE CYCLE	AVERAGE HEIGHT	PROPAGATION METHOD
*bay	[TP]	2' to 6'	5
lemon balm	P	18"	4/2
salad burnet	P	18"	2
Roman chamomile	P	6"	1
*chives	P	12"	1
*marjoram	TP	12"	1
MINTS:			
peppermint	P	24"	4
*spearmint	P	18"	4
*oregano	P	12" to 24"	4
*rosemary	[TP]	12" to 24"	5
*sage	P	24"	5
sorrel	P	18"	3
*tarragon	P	18" to 24"	4

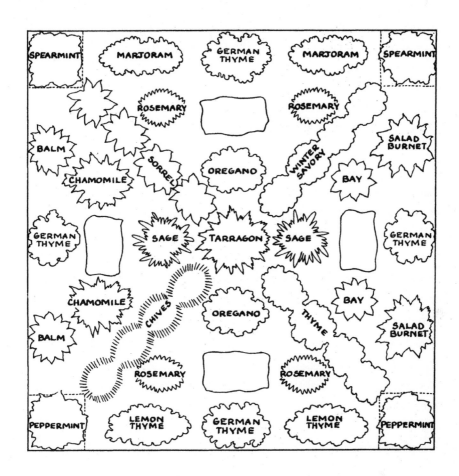

HERB	LIFE CYCLE	AVERAGE HEIGHT	PROPAGATION METHOD
THYMES:			
*thyme	P	12"	4
German thyme	P	12"	1
lemon thyme	P	6"	4
winter savory	P	12"	2

Mint Garden

THIS PLAN IS FOR people who want the full range of mint flavors. Installing the extra dividers, using 2" x 10" or 2" x 12" lumber cut to size, is a bother initially, but it pays off over the years. It's the only sane way to grow a variety of mints in the same bed.

Keep cutting back all the mints throughout the growing season. If you let two or more go to flower, the bees will cause cross-pollination and your varieties will get even more varied and lose some of their distinctive flavor. Harvest 4" to 6" off the stems every other week during the summer. If you can't use all the clippings immediately, hang them to dry, then store in glass jars in a pantry or kitchen cabinet. They'll last through winter for all your mint needs.

The drawback to continuous cutting is that it stimulates root growth in plants that naturally spread like wildfire in the first place. In 2 or 3 years, each mint will become overcrowded in its 2' x 2' growing area and need to be subdivided and started anew.

There are dozens of different varieties of mint. The ones included here have been most popular among my customers, who use them chiefly in teas, cold drinks, fruit salads, and jellies.

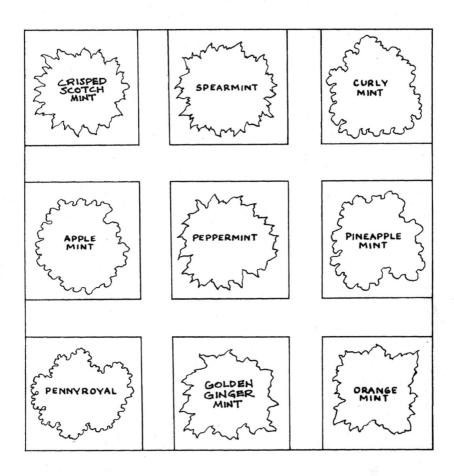

HERB	LIFE CYCLE	AVERAGE HEIGHT	PROPAGATION METHOD
apple	P	24"	4
crisped Scotch	P	18"	4
curly	P	24"	4
golden ginger	P	18"	4
orange	P	16"	4
pennyroyal	P	3"	3
peppermint	P	24"	4
pineapple	P	12"	4
*spearmint	P	18"	4

Sage Garden

SAGE IS A NATURAL COLLECTOR'S item because it comes in so many varieties (there are at least 500 known members of the species) and offers so many contrasts in color of foliage and flower. Many of the varieties also tend to "sport"—a horticultural quirk whereby different colors appear in leaves or flowers on the same plant. Every year I get at least one common gray sage that is gray-green on one side of the leaf, as it is supposed to be, and pure white on the other, as though someone had touched it up with a paintbrush.

The sages included in this plan are among the showiest of those varieties that are most readily available.

Most sages get big quickly, which is why they are given so much garden space here. They must also be trimmed from time to time, especially after the second season, when unchecked growth would diminish the aesthetic effect of the garden.

In propagating the gold, purple, and tricolor from cuttings, pick sprigs with the most desirable color variations in their leaves, so that this characteristic carries over into the new plant.

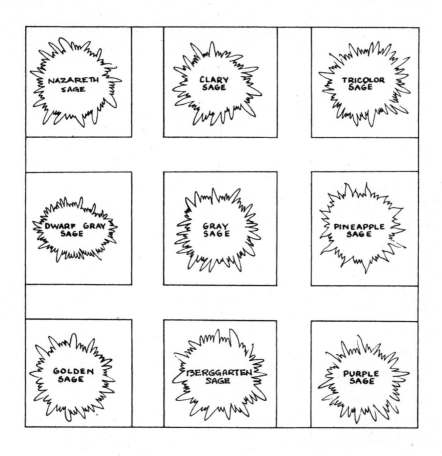

HERB	LIFE CYCLE	AVERAGE HEIGHT	PROPAGATION METHOD
*gray sage	P	24"	5
Berggarten	[P]	12"	5
clary	B	4'	2
dwarf gray	[TP]	8"	5
golden	P	15"	5
Nazareth	P	12"	5
pineapple	TP	30" to 36"	5
purple	P	15"	5
tricolor	P	15"	5

Thyme Garden

THE CLOCK PATTERN of this plan takes several years to fully develop and needs a lot of attention to trimming. Two low-growing creeping varieties—woolly and white or white-flowering—have been used to define the main areas. You could use bricks to frame the clock face from the start; otherwise, trim and train the woolly and white-flowering thymes to get the same effect gradually.

The clock can be "set" for any time, of course—the hour of a special birth, say, or one associated with a cherished occasion.

Most thymes are perennials, but there are variations in their degrees of hardiness, so it's a good idea to winter-mulch the entire thyme garden in northern areas.

It's possible to start a few thymes from seed, such as common English, French, and German, but most of them must be propagated by division or cutting. In cases where the color or color variegation is a special feature, take cuttings that best represent that feature.

Woolly thyme varieties are especially prone to fungus disease in wet periods. If your plants start rotting, cut them back severely to promote new, healthy growth.

Thyme is one of the most popular herbs to grow. If you're going to try to build a collection of thymes, though, be prepared for a challenge and some frustration, because there is rampant confusion in the naming and labeling of the varieties. I've ordered what turned out to be the same variety of thyme under six or seven different names on several occasions. This is partly due to the subtle ways in which many of the varieties differ. In fact, in a half-century of growing this herb, I think I have finally learned to recognize and identify for certain only about twenty varieties.

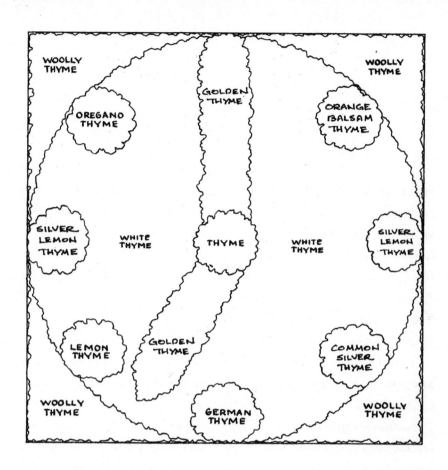

HERB	LIFE CYCLE	AVERAGE HEIGHT	PROPAGATION METHOD
*thyme	P	12"	1
German	P	12"	1
golden	[P]	8"	5
lemon	P	6"	4
orange balsam	P	8"	5
oregano	P	8"	5
silver lemon	[P]	8"	5
white	P	1"	4
woolly	P	1"	4

Basil Garden

HERE'S THE PERFECT GARDEN for supplying all the basil a small Italian restaurant will need. Actually, most traditional Italian families with garden space grow at least a half-dozen basil varieties. Few cooks seem to agree as to which variety makes the best pesto sauce, however. Most Italians believe that Genovese varieties from the Genoa area in Italy are the best. I've learned to stay out of arguments on the subject, but when pressed, over a glass of homemade red wine, I usually say that the smaller the basil leaf, the better the pesto flavor.

In this plan the basils have been arranged in rows, crop-style, with the tall-growing sacred and Aussie Sweetie varieties in the middle.

Among the small-leaved basils (dwarf and fine-leaf varieties) there is always some variation in growth pattern. If I were to raise a dozen plants of one type from seeds, I'd seldom get more than three plants that look exactly alike. They'd range in leaf length from ⅛" to ⅜" and in height from 8" to 12".

HERB	LIFE CYCLE	AVERAGE HEIGHT	PROPAGATION METHOD
*basil (common or bush)	A	18"	2
Aussie Sweetie	A	30"	2
dwarf	A	12"	2
fine-leaf	A	15"	2
lemon	A	15"	2
lettuce-leaf	A	18"	2
purple opal	A	18"	2
sacred	A	30"	2

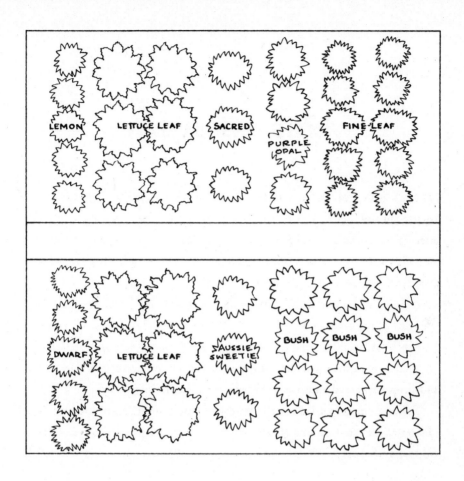

The labels in the illustration read:

LEMON, LETTUCE LEAF, SACRED, PURPLE OPAL, FINE LEAF

DWARF, LETTUCE LEAF, AUSSIE SWEETIE, BUSH, BUSH, BUSH

Allium Garden

THE LOWLY ONION can make one of the most attractive and easy-to-care-for gardens of all. This one is arranged crop-style, with the 3- to 4-foot-high Globemaster in the corners. Started from bulbs or seedlings, the chives, Molly, Welsh onion, and roseum, if allowed to flower, will bloom in purple, yellow, white, and pink, respectively.

The Globemaster, Molly, and roseum are mainly decorative and not usually used in cooking.

The leeks and onions are harvested in full in the fall and need to be replaced with new crops in the spring. For bigger and better heads of garlic, plant the cloves in the fall.

The onion family grows much better in a sweet, moderately enriched soil. This garden should be well-limed and composted or manured for maximum productivity.

HERB	LIFE CYCLE	AVERAGE HEIGHT	PROPAGATION METHOD
CHIVES:			
*chives	P	12"	1
curly	P	6"	4
garlic	P	12"	4
Globemaster	P	36"	bulb
Molly	P	12"	bulb
roseum	P	15"	bulb

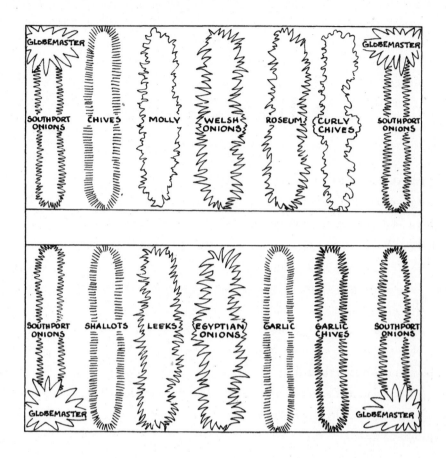

HERB	LIFE CYCLE	AVERAGE HEIGHT	PROPAGATION METHOD
garlic	P	24"	bulb
leeks	P	24"	1
Egyptian onions	P	24"	bulb
Southport onions	B	18"	1
Welsh onions	P	18"	4
shallots	P	12"	bulb

Salad Garden

THE SALAD HERBS have been planted in rows rather than spot-planted, so this looks more like a vegetable garden than an herb garden. Annuals and perennials are separated by the divider. The sorrel, roquette, cress, and dandelion can be used in place of lettuce as well as with lettuce in many salads. The other herbs are used to accent salads and many other dishes, too. Make sure to keep picking salad herbs during the summer so they don't go to seed. If any of the annuals get ahead of you and begin to toughen, pull them up and sow new seed.

HERB	LIFE CYCLE	AVERAGE HEIGHT	PROPAGATION METHOD
*basil	A	18"	2
salad burnet	P	18"	2
chervil	A	12"	3
*chives	P	12"	1
corn salad	A	8"	3
garden cress	A	6"	3
dandelion	P	4"	3
nasturtium	A	8"	3
*parsley	B	8"	3
roquette	A	10"	3
winter savory	P	12"	2
sorrel	P	18"	3

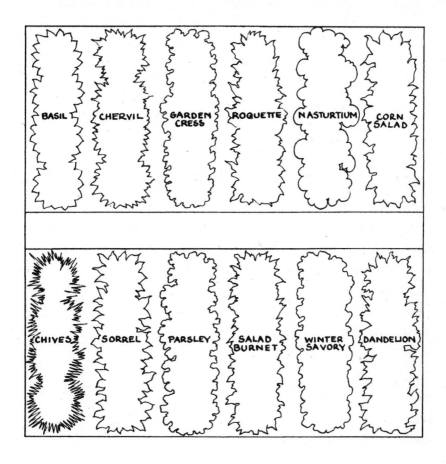

Tea Garden

MANY MORE HERBS can be used to make teas than the ones given in this plan; the type and quantity of the selection here simply reflect our own tea tastes. Comfrey, hyssop, lemon verbena, and dozens of other herbs are also quite popular. There are different opinions as to the best way to prepare libations of herbal tea. I use a tablespoon of fresh herbs (or a teaspoon of dried herbs) per cup of boiling water and let steep for about 10 minutes. But I know people who advocate the use of hot but not boiling water, and who steep the tea for shorter intervals. Blends of herbs can also be as tasty as single-herb teas.

HERB	LIFE CYCLE	AVERAGE HEIGHT	PROPAGATION METHOD
anise	A	24"	3
basil	A	18"	2
lemon basil	A	18"	2
bee balm	P	30"	4
borage	A	30"	2
burnet	P	18"	2
calendula	A	24"	2/3
chamomile	A	18" to 24"	2
caraway	B	24"	2
catnip	P	18"	1/4
fennel	A	30"	3
lemon balm	P	18"	4/2

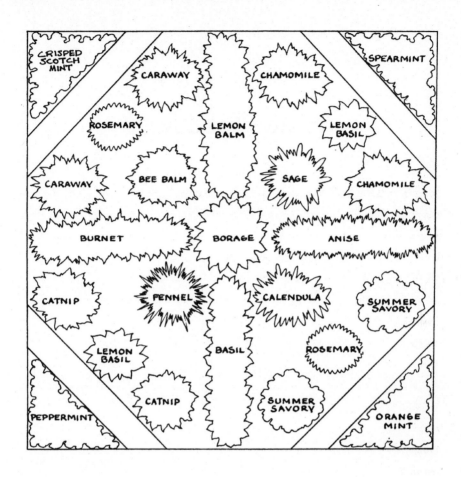

HERB	LIFE CYCLE	AVERAGE HEIGHT	PROPAGATION METHOD
MINTS:			
crisped Scotch	P	18"	4
orange	P	24"	4
peppermint	P	24"	4
*spearmint	P	18"	4
*rosemary	[TP]	12" to 24"	5
*sage	P	24"	5
*summer savory	A	18"	3

Soup Garden

AMONG MY CUSTOMERS, these are the most popular herbs used in making and seasoning soups. The lovage in the center will grow up to 6' even if you keep trimming it, so if you're not sure you'll use this herb, eliminate it as a center plant and fill in with more sorrel instead.

HERB	LIFE CYCLE	AVERAGE HEIGHT	PROPAGATION METHOD
*basil	A	18"	2
*bay	[TP]	2' to 6'	5
borage	A	30"	2
caraway	B	24"	2
*chives	P	12"	1
*dill	A	30"	3
garlic	P	24"	bulb
leeks	P	24"	1
lemon balm	P	18"	4/2
lovage	P	6'	2
*marjoram	TP	12"	1
*parsley	B	8"	3
*rosemary	[TP]	12" to 24"	5
*sage	P	24"	5
winter savory	P	12"	2
sorrel	P	18"	3
*tarragon	P	18" to 24"	4
*thyme	P	12"	1

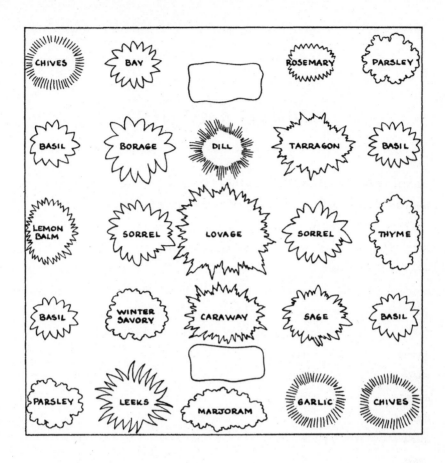

Bread Garden

ONLY A SMALL QUANTITY of any of these herbs, fresh or dried, is needed to give a delightful flavor to loaves of home-baked bread.

The rows of saffron, or autumn crocus, can make this a lovely and enduring garden. In the first year, start everything except the saffron in the spring. Then, around Labor Day, plant the saffron from bulbs, which will be readily available in good garden centers at that time. In about 6 weeks, the saffron will flower, and you can collect the precious orange stigma, which are used for flavoring. Thereafter, the saffron will flower beautifully every fall without any more work on your part.

HERB	LIFE CYCLE	AVERAGE HEIGHT	PROPAGATION METHOD
basil	A	15"	2
caraway	B	24"	2
*coriander	A	24"	2
cress	A	6"	3
*dill	A	30"	3
fennel	A	30"	3
*marjoram	TP	12"	1
poppy	A	18" to 36"	2
*rosemary	[TP]	12" to 24"	5
*saffron	P	6"	bulb
*sage	P	24"	5
*thyme	P	12"	1

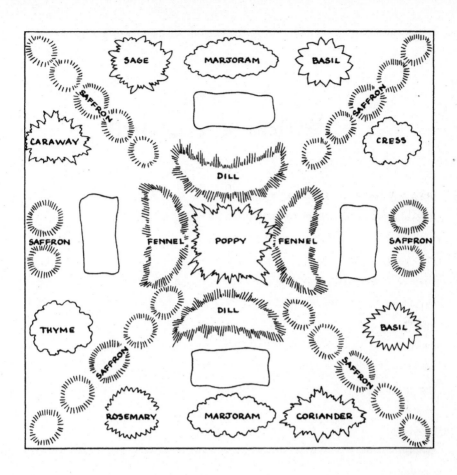

Breakfast Garden

FOR LOVERS OF OMELETS (or scrambled eggs), here is a garden that will permit great variety in the flavor of your breakfasts and brunches. It doubles as a salad garden.

HERB	LIFE CYCLE	AVERAGE HEIGHT	PROPAGATION METHOD
dwarf basil	A	12"	2
*chives	P	12"	1
cress	A	6"	3
*dill	A	30"	3
*marjoram	TP	12"	1
mustard	A	18"	3
onions	B	18" to 24"	1/bulb
*parsley	B	8"	3
*rosemary	[TP]	12" to 24"	5
*summer savory	A	24"	3
*tarragon	P	18" to 24"	4
*thyme	P	12"	1

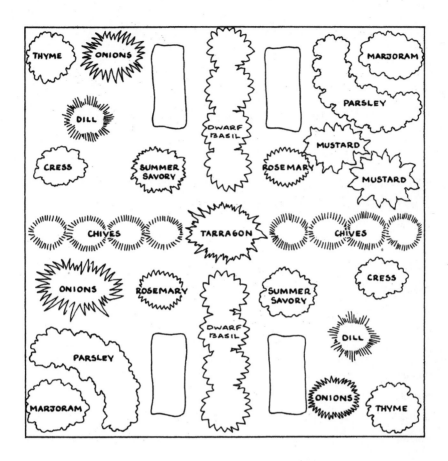

Fish & Game Garden

HERE'S A FUNCTIONAL LAYOUT of the herb seasonings most commonly used to temper strong-tasting fish dishes and meals made from wild fowl, venison, and such.

HERB	LIFE CYCLE	AVERAGE HEIGHT	PROPAGATION METHOD
lemon basil	A	15"	2
*bay	[TP]	2' to 6'	5
*dill	A	30"	3
fennel	A	30"	3
garlic	P	24"	bulb
hyssop	P	24"	2
*marjoram	[TP]	12"	1
onions	B	18" to 24"	1/bulb
*oregano	P	12" to 24"	4
*parsley	B	8"	3
*rosemary	[TP]	12" to 24"	5
*sage	P	24"	5
*summer savory	A	18" to 24"	3
shallots	P	12"	bulb
*tarragon	P	18" to 24"	4
*thyme	P	12"	1
caraway thyme	P	1"	5

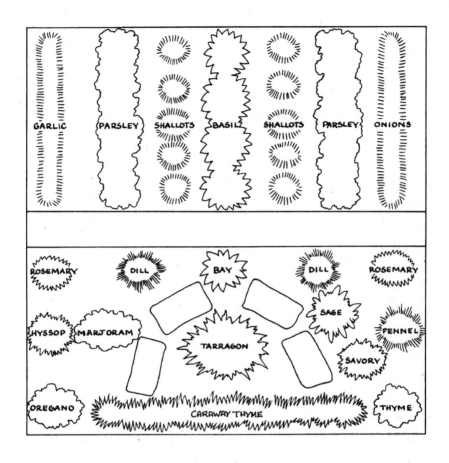

Cake & Cookie Garden

THIS PLAN CONTAINS the herbs whose leaves and seeds are frequently used as ingredients in dessert dishes.

HERB	LIFE CYCLE	AVERAGE HEIGHT	PROPAGATION METHOD
anise	A	24"	3
caraway	B	24"	2
*coriander	A	24"	2
costmary	P	36"	4
fennel	A	30"	3
MINTS:			
orange	P	24"	4
*spearmint	P	18"	4
poppy	A	24"	2
stevia	TP	24"	2
SCENTED GERANIUMS:			
apple	[A]	12"	5
nutmeg	[A]	18"	5

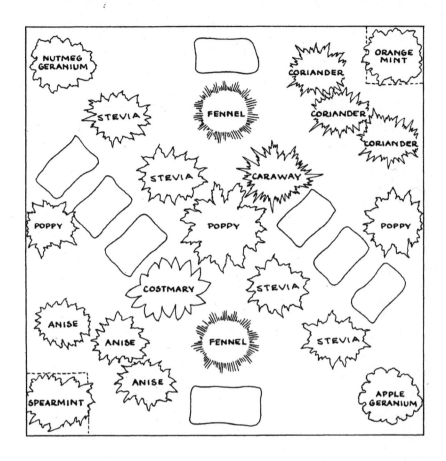

Home Bar Garden

THIS MIGHT BE A POPULAR GARDEN off a porch or patio for folks who make libations an important part of their entertaining. Some of these herbs are best used fresh to flavor iced drinks; others are traditionally used to give a distinctive taste to homemade wines and liqueurs.

The mints and lemon verbena should be confined, or can be raised in large containers, such as whiskey barrels, partly to convey the personality of the garden, but also to help these herbs grow their best. The sweet woodruff in the center will do well only if something like a barrel or umbrella is there to keep it shaded; otherwise you should plant this May wine ingredient in a naturally shady spot.

HERB	LIFE CYCLE	AVERAGE HEIGHT	PROPAGATION METHOD
anise	A	24"	3
caraway	B	24"	2
*coriander	A	24"	2
horseradish	P	24"	4
fennel	A	30"	3
lemon balm	P	18"	4/2
lemon verbena	[A]	4' to 6'	5
MINTS:			
peppermint	P	24"	4
*spearmint	P	18"	4
Roman wormwood	P	18"	4
sweet woodruff	P	6"	4/5
tansy	P	36"	4

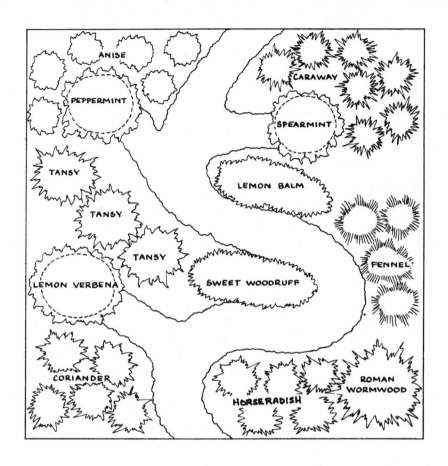

Potpourri Garden

THE EMPHASIS IN THIS PLAN is on the herbs most frequently used to make dried potpourris. Leaves (and rose petals) should be harvested, dried, and stored in a sealed, opaque container. If a few drops of fixative are added, the mixture will retain its potency much longer.

A hybrid tea rose would be the best choice for the center plant here; other types of roses get too big for the space available.

HERB	LIFE CYCLE	AVERAGE HEIGHT	PROPAGATION METHOD
ambrosia	A	18"	2/3
lemon balm	P	18”	4/2
*basil	A	18"	2
eucalyptus	[TP]	6'	2
rose geranium	A	24"	5
lavender	P	18"	2/5
*marjoram	[TP]	12"	1
pennyroyal mint	P	3"	3
rose	P	4'	–
*rosemary	[TP]	12" to 24"	5
rue	P	24"	2
*sage	P	24"	5
sweet myrtle	[TP]	18"	5
orange balsam thyme	P	8"	5
violets	P	4"	3/4

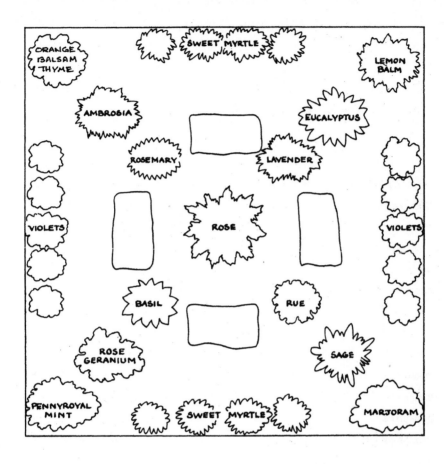

Pest Repellent Garden

HERE ARE SOME HERBS FREQUENTLY USED IN companion planting to deter pests in vegetable gardens. I'm not an advocate of companion planting in vegetable plots of limited space, simply because the method robs crop space. But I do believe in the underlying principle; in fact, I make my own organic pesticides by harvesting the leaves and/or flowers of the herbs featured, chopping them in a blender, letting the concoction sit overnight in some water, then straining and spraying on the plants with bug problems.

HERB	LIFE CYCLE	AVERAGE HEIGHT	PROPAGATION METHOD	DETERS
hyssop	P	24"	2	white fly
marigolds	A	15"	2	nematodes
nasturtium	A	12"	3	aphid, thrips
pyrethrum	P	18"	2	mites, aphid, leafhopper
rue	P	24"	2	beetles
santolina	P	12"	5	aphid, white fly
tansy	P	36"	4	ants
lemon thyme	P	6"	4	fleas, flies, mosquitoes

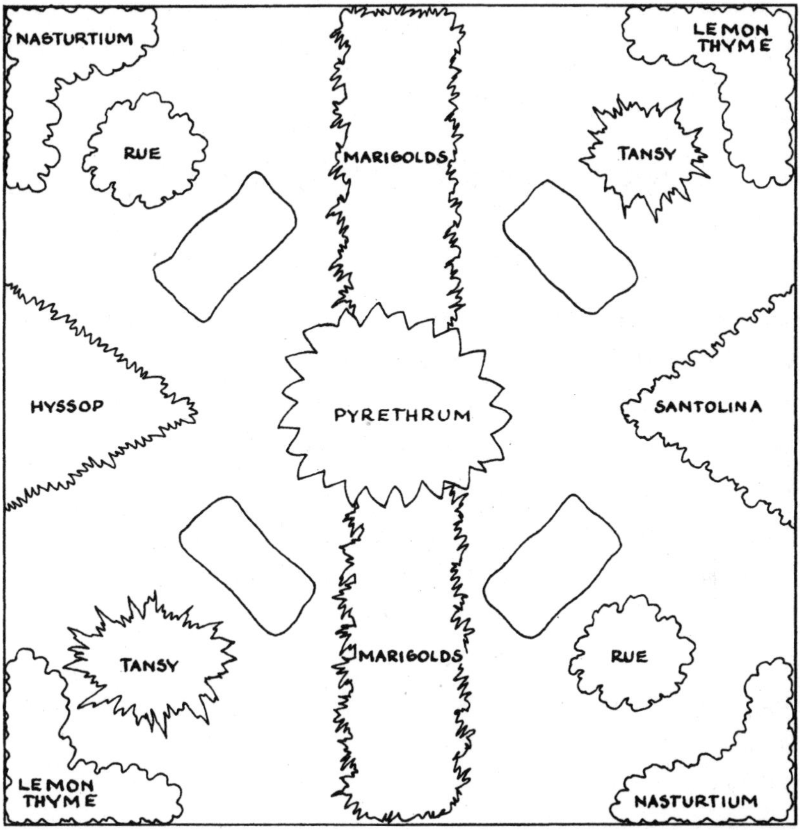
NASTURTIUM
LEMON THYME
RUE
MARIGOLDS
TANSY
HYSSOP
PYRETHRUM
SANTOLINA
TANSY
MARIGOLDS
RUE
LEMON THYME
NASTURTIUM

Pest Repellent Garden

Honeybee Garden

THESE MOST AROMATIC HERBS are favorites of bees and beekeepers. The borage areas should be sown in succession, at about 2-week intervals, to maximize the appeal of that herb's blossoms for bees. All the other plants in the garden should be chopped back as soon as the blooms begin to fade and fall—to encourage new flowering and continued bee traffic.

HERB	LIFE CYCLE	AVERAGE HEIGHT	PROPAGATION METHOD
bee balm (red)	P	30"	4
sacred basil	A	30"	2
borage	A	30"	2
chamomile	A	18" to 24"	2
catnip	P	18"	1/4
fennel	A	30"	3
hyssop	P	24"	2
lavender	P	15"	2/5
lemon balm	P	18"	4/2
*marjoram	TP	12"	1
MINTS:			
peppermint	P	24"	4
*spearmint	P	18"	4
*oregano	P	12" to 24"	4
*sage	P	24"	5
winter savory	P	12"	2
*thyme	P	12"	1

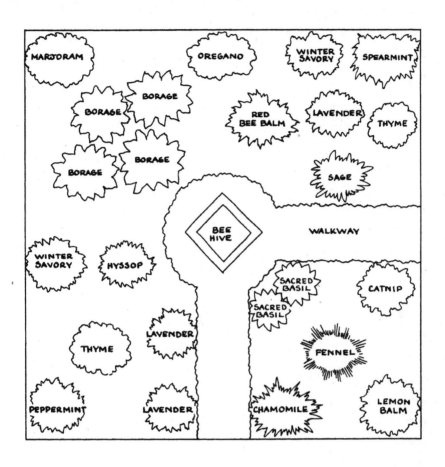

Medicinal Herb Garden

THIS PLAN CONSISTS of some of the herbs commonly used in a variety of popular herbal remedies.

HERB	LIFE CYCLE	AVERAGE HEIGHT	PROPAGATION METHOD
chamomile	A	18"	2
catnip	P	18"	1/4
cayenne pepper	A	30"	2
comfrey	P	36"	4
foxglove	B	36"	2
garlic	P	24"	bulb
horehound	P	18"	2
horseradish	P	24"	4
mullein	B	4' to 6'	2
peppermint	P	24"	4
black peppermint	P	18"	4
*rosemary	[TP]	12" to 24"	5
rue	P	24"	2
*sage	P	24"	5

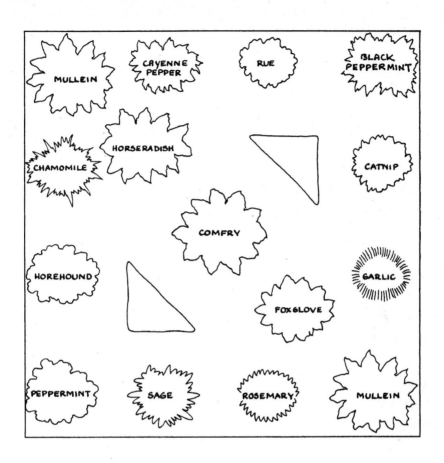

MULLEIN

CAYENNE PEPPER

RUE

BLACK PEPPERMINT

HORSERADISH

CHAMOMILE

CATNIP

COMFRY

HOREHOUND

GARLIC

FOXGLOVE

PEPPERMINT

SAGE

ROSEMARY

MULLEIN

Dyer's Garden

THERE HAS BEEN A TREMENDOUS increase in interest in using natural colors among people who make their own clothes and textiles. This plan offers a representative selection of herbs that can be easily grown for dyeing purposes. All the plants here grow big and tall, so no particular effort has been made to design the garden. Yet this or any other garden of dye plants will be most attractive.

Here are some good dye sources for specific colors from among herbs mentioned in this book (not all of them appear in this particular garden):

Yellow: lady's bedstraw, dyer's broom, dyer's chamomile, safflower, saffron, St. John's wort

Green: motherwort

Red: lady's bedstraw (roots), madder, rue (roots), wild marjoram

Dark Yellow/Gold: marigold

Tan/Gold: orange osage

Brass/Burnt Orange: onion

Yellow/Green: tansy, nettle, sorrel

Blue: woad, elecampane

Magenta: dandelion

HERB	LIFE CYCLE	AVERAGE HEIGHT	PROPAGATION METHOD
dyer's broom	P	18"	2
elecampane	P	12" to 24"	4
lady's bedstraw	P	24"	2
madder	P	12"	4
wild marjoram	P	18"	1

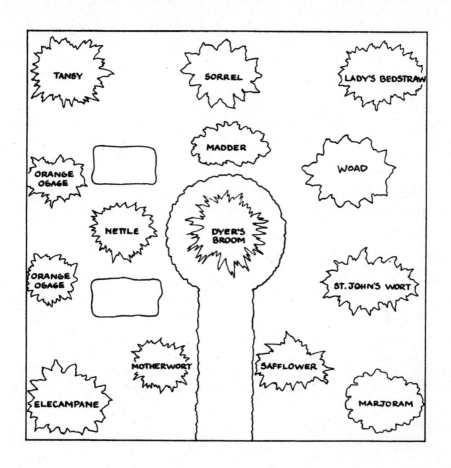

HERB	LIFE CYCLE	AVERAGE HEIGHT	PROPAGATION METHOD
motherwort	P	30"	2
nettle	P	24"	3
orange osage	[P]	6'	2
St. John's wort	P	18"	3
safflower	A	24"	2
sorrel	P	18"	3
tansy	P	36"	4
woad	B	36"	3

Colonial Garden

THESE ARE THE HERBS that were most commonly included in eighteenth-century kitchen gardens for their everyday culinary, medicinal, and dyeing usages. The herbs in the center have been planted within the spokes of an old wagon wheel.

HERB	LIFE CYCLE	AVERAGE HEIGHT	PROPAGATION METHOD
*basil	A	18"	2
bee balm	P	30"	4
calendula	A	24"	2/3
catnip	P	18"	1/4
comfrey	P	36"	4
costmary	P	36"	4
foxglove	B	36"	2
hyssop	P	24"	2
lady's mantle	P	12"	4
lavender	P	18"	2/5
lemon balm	P	18"	4/2
*marjoram	TP	12"	1
pennyroyal mint	P	3"	3
nasturtium	A	8"	3
rue	P	24"	2

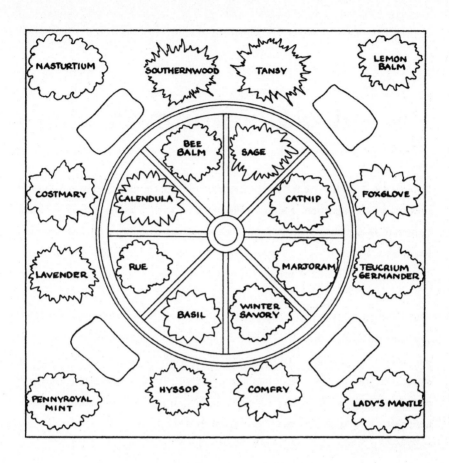

HERB	LIFE CYCLE	AVERAGE HEIGHT	PROPAGATION METHOD
*sage	P	24"	5
winter savory	P	12"	2
southernwood	P	36"	4
tansy	P	36"	4
teucrium germander	P	15"	5

Scented Geranium Garden

THIS IS A POPULAR TYPE of garden because there are so many scented geraniums to pick from—about 200 varieties, with a wide range of leaf patterns, growing habits, and rose, fruit, or spice aromas—and because they make excellent houseplants and so can be brought indoors for the winter in northern areas. Like the mints, thymes, and sages, they are a natural collector's item.

Geraniums are tough to start from seed. Seed is available, but it's expensive and sometimes does not come out true to the type on the label even if you do succeed in getting it to sprout. An alternative for collecting rare varieties is to order them as young plants through the mail. If you do this, buy from suppliers no more than 2 to 3 shipping days away, or have them shipped by air. Otherwise the plants are likely to perish in transit.

If you can't buy plants close to home, the next best way to propagate is by taking cuttings off a friend's established plants in spring for development in a bright window. They are harder to start from cuttings than their cousins, the familiar bright-flowering geraniums, because they are highly susceptible to rotting due to their high essential oil content. Therefore, be sure to use a well-drained sand/perlite rooting medium and to water conservatively during the 4 weeks that most cuttings will require before rooting. Be especially careful not to get the cuttings wet on cloudy days. Select sprigs that are tender, but neither too soft nor too woody. Once rooted, transplant into standard planting medium in 4" peat pots and sink the pots in the garden (after danger of frost is past).

The garden plan here includes large growing types, such as the peppermint geranium, and compact growers like French lace. It reflects the three types of scents—rose (of which there are over fifty varieties), fruit, and spice.

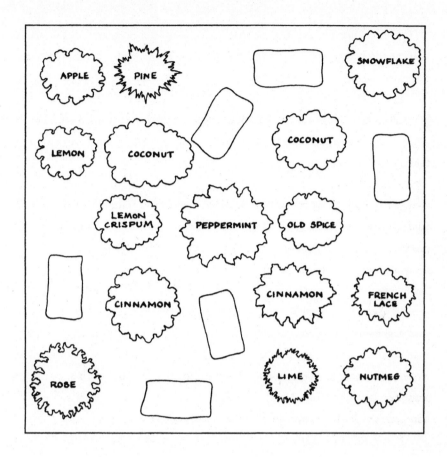

And it has a sampling of the main growing styles—the upright, such as lemon crispum; the trailing, such as coconut; and the bushy, such as nutmeg or pine.

Smaller-growing scented geraniums can be brought inside at the end of the growing season: dig up and pot, trimming off any larger, more unruly branches. If you have kept them trimmed throughout the summer (leaves can be used for making jams and jellies or potpourris, or for floating on your bath water), most will remain small enough to be brought inside without too much fuss. Unlike almost all the other herbs, scented geraniums do not require a window with a full sunny southern exposure. They do well in any window with as little as 4 hours of sun. They'll remain semidormant until early March, when they'll begin to put forth new growth again.

For convenience, and also to spare your plant unnecessary root damage, you can plant your smaller geraniums in 6" to 8" pots when you first set them out into the garden in the spring.

The larger-growing varieties—in this plan, the rose, snowflake, and peppermint—simply get too big in the garden to bring indoors intact. If you want any of them for company over the winter, start them from cuttings taken off the established plant in late summer.

HERB	LIFE CYCLE	AVERAGE HEIGHT	PROPAGATION METHOD
apple	[A]	12"	5
cinnamon	[A]	18"	5
coconut	[A]	15"	5
French lace	[A]	18"	5
lemon	[A]	24"	5
lemon crispum	[A]	24"	5
lime	[A]	18"	5
nutmeg	[A]	18"	5
old spice	[A]	18"	5
peppermint	A	24"	5
pine	[A]	18"	5
rose	A	24"	5
snowflake	A	24"	5

White-Flowering Herb Garden

IN THIS AND THE THREE PLANS that follow, the herbs are selected primarily for the colors of their blossoms and are separated by distance—the whites from the blues, and the blues from the reds, and the reds from the yellow—for a couple of reasons.

First, it provides an easy reference for gardeners interested in quickly finding out which herbs produce blossoms of a particular color.

Also, it makes sense botanically to keep some herb families separated by color. If you tried to grow all three shades of hyssop together, for example, cross-pollination would eventually spoil your effort, and you might end up with only one diluted color.

Most of the perennial herbs will not reach blossoming stage until the second year. Some perennials will flower the first year in regions with longer growing seasons if transplanted into the garden early enough in the spring.

In any case, none of the perennials stay in flower for more than 2 or 3 weeks. They should be cut back as soon as the blooms are finished to foster new growth and a possible second flowering.

Of course, if you're cutting stems and leaves continuously for other uses, you won't see any flowers.

Two pretty white-flowering herbs are not included in this first plan: angelica because it gets too large for a garden of this size, and sweet woodruff because it only thrives in shade.

HERB	LIFE CYCLE	AVERAGE HEIGHT	PROPAGATION METHOD
anise	A	24"	3
salad burnet	P	18"	2
chamomile	A	24"	2
caraway	B	24"	2
*chervil	A	12"	2
horehound	P	18"	2
hyssop (white)	P	24"	2
*marjoram	TP	12"	1
poppy	A	24" to 36"	2
white thyme	P	1"	4

Order of Flowering

First Year:

chamomile, thyme, chervil, anise, marjoram (possibly), hyssop (possibly)

Subsequent Years:

caraway, burnet, poppy, chamomile, chervil, thyme, marjoram, horehound, hyssop, anise

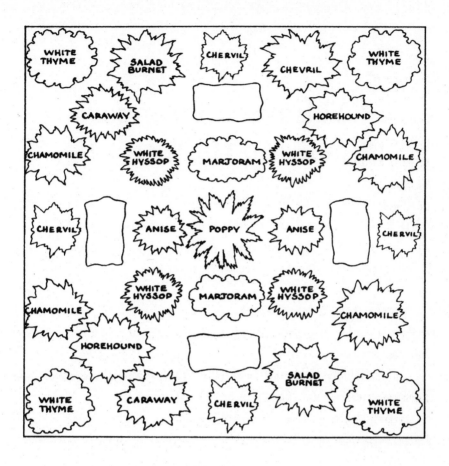

White-Flowering Herb Garden

Yellow- & Orange-Flowering Herb Garden

THIS GARDEN IS AS GOOD a cutting garden as any, and beginning in July you can regularly bring in bunches of various daisy-shaped flowers. It is the boldest, tallest-growing, and potentially most productive of all the flowering herb gardens.

Mustard, fennel, and a few of the common culinary herbs will also flower yellow when let go to seed, but they are not included here because their blooms are nothing special.

Dill is included because its umbrella-shaped flower is so attractive and works so effectively in bouquets or dried arrangements.

HERB	LIFE CYCLE	AVERAGE HEIGHT	PROPAGATION METHOD
calendula	A	24"	2/3
costmary	P	36"	4
*dill	A	30"	3
dyer's chamomile	P	30"	2
fern-leaf tansy	P	24"	4
lady's bedstraw	P	12" to 24"	2
marigolds	A	15"	2
nasturtium	A	8"	3
saffron	P	6"	bulb
yarrow	P	24"	2/4

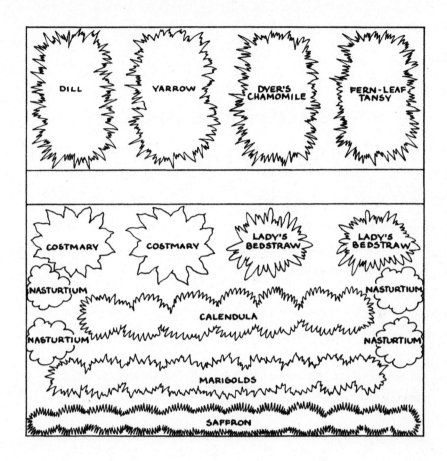

Order of Flowering

First Year:

marigolds, calendula, nasturtium, dill, tansy, saffron

Subsequent Years:

marigolds, yarrow, calendula, nasturtium, lady's bedstraw, costmary, dill, tansy, saffron

Pink- & Red-Flowering Herb Garden

EXCEPT FOR THE PINEAPPLE SAGE, all these herbs are hardy perennials. As with the preceding flower plans, they could do equally well planted in border areas or as cutting gardens in the yard.

HERB	LIFE CYCLE	AVERAGE HEIGHT	PROPAGATION METHOD
bee balm (red, pink, or scarlet)	P	30"	4
pineapple sage	TP	30"	5
pink hyssop	P	24"	2
wild marjoram	P	24"	4
pink thyme	P	3"	4
red creeping thyme	P	3"	4
red valerian	P	3'	4
yarrow (red or pink)	P	24"	2/4

Order of Flowering

First Year:

thymes, bee balm, pineapple sage, hyssop, wild marjoram, red valerian, yarrow

Subsequent Years:

thymes, bee balm, hyssop, wild marjoram, pineapple sage, yarrow, red valerian

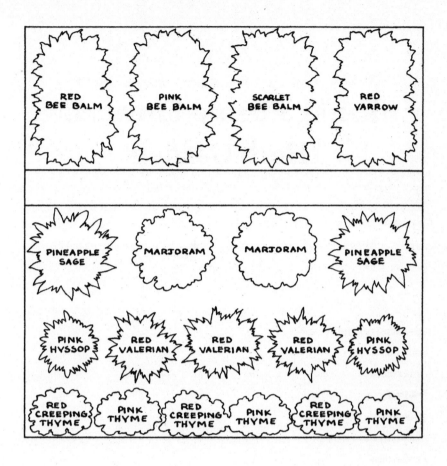

Blue- & Purple-Flowering Herb Garden

WITH THE EXCEPTION OF BORAGE and heliotrope, all the herbs in this garden of subtle, rather than dramatic, blue- and purple-flowering herbs are perennials.

HERB	LIFE CYCLE	AVERAGE HEIGHT	PROPAGATION METHOD
bee balm (lavender)	P	30"	4
borage	A	30"	2
catnip mussini	P	18"	4
heliotrope	[A]	18"	5/2
blue hyssop	P	24"	2
lavender Vera	P	18"	5/2
Korean mint	P	30"	2
rosemary	[TP]	12" to 24"	5
sage	P	24"	5
woolly thyme	P	1"	4

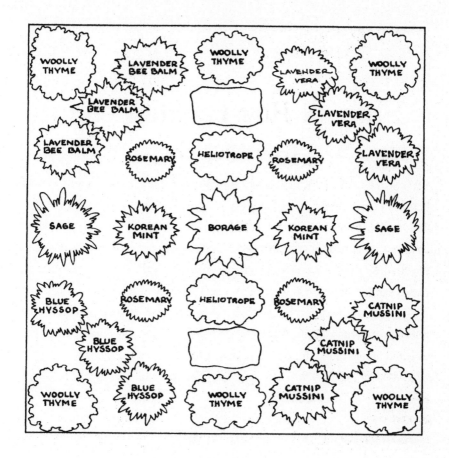

Order of Flowering

First Year:

  borage, heliotrope, thyme, catnip, Korean mint

Subsequent Years:

  borage, heliotrope, woolly thyme, hyssop, catnip mussini, bee balm, rosemary, lavender, sage, Korean mint

Silver Garden

THIS GARDEN CREATES an exquisite effect in midsummer. The sun brings out the subtle variations in gray and silver in the plants and also the delicate differences in the various leaf shapes and growing patterns. It doesn't require a great deal of attention—certainly nowhere near the time and effort required by the basic culinary garden—yet the results can be stunning. The plants can be cut in fall and saved for use in dried arrangements in the winter.

During wet weather, the artemisias—silver king, silver queen, and silver mound—are fungus-prone. If rotting develops, cut away bad parts of the affected plants to promote new, healthy growth.

HERB	LIFE CYCLE	AVERAGE HEIGHT	PROPAGATION METHOD
ARTEMISIAS:			
Roman wormwood	P	18"	4
silver king	P	24" to 36"	4
silver mound	P	6"	4
silver queen	P	24"	4
versicolor	P	15"	4/5
curry	P	15"	5
dittany of Crete	[A]	10"	5
eucalyptus	[TP]	4' to 6'	2
horehound	P	18"	2

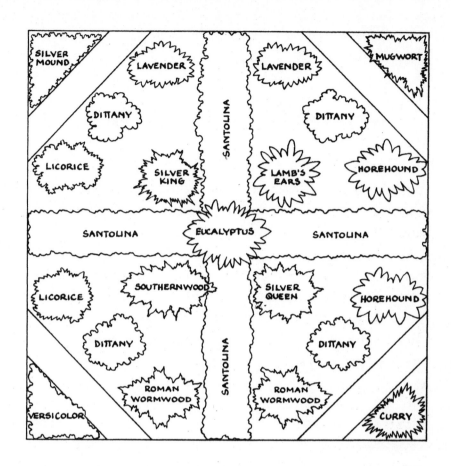

HERB	LIFE CYCLE	AVERAGE HEIGHT	PROPAGATION METHOD
lamb's ears	P	12"	4
lavender	P	18"	2/5
licorice	[A]	12"	5
mugwort	P	3'	2/4
santolina	P	12"	5
southernwood	P	3'	4

Christmas Wreath Garden

LIKE THE CLOCK-SHAPED thyme garden, this garden takes several years to develop fully in the yard, but you can gather material for a homemade herbal Christmas wreath from it beginning in the first year.

Most of the space in this garden is devoted to the santolina, because I think it's the best prime herb material for wreath-making. Artemisias can be planted and used in this quantity instead, but, when dried, they have a tendency to get too brittle to work with easily. Statice is another common base material for wreaths. It's easy to work with, but it is not an attractive grower in small gardens—it gets too weedy—so I've left it out altogether.

HERB	LIFE CYCLE	AVERAGE HEIGHT	PROPAGATION METHOD
*bay	[TP]	2' to 6'	5
lavender	P	24"	2/5
*rosemary	[TP]	12" to 24"	5
santolina	P	12"	5
silver king	P	24"	4
silver thyme	[P]	8"	5
wormwood	P	24" to 36"	2/4
yarrow	P	24"	2/4

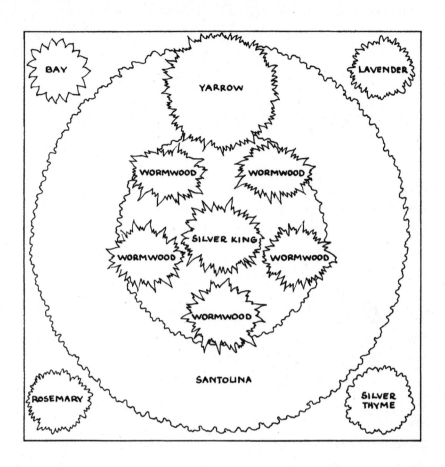

Shady Garden

THIS PLAN, FOR AREAS THAT GET less than 4 hours of sun a day, is popular with people who have a lot of trees to contend with in their gardens. It will not work in dense shade where only mushrooms grow, however. Some of the herbs included here—parsley, tarragon, cress, and salad burnet—also do well in full sun. The others perform their best in less than full sunlight.

Ginseng and goldenseal are two shade-loving herbs not included in this plan because they require unusual soil conditions. They do best in a sloping natural woodland setting where there is lots of drainage yet plenty of leaf mold in the ground.

Angelica, a biennial that does well in shade, isn't included because it grows to such a large size that by the second year it would overwhelm this small area.

HERB	LIFE CYCLE	AVERAGE HEIGHT	PROPAGATION METHOD
salad burnet	P	18"	2
*chervil	A	12"	2
costmary	P	36"	6
garden cress	A	6"	3
lemon balm	P	18"	4/2
*parsley	B	8"	3

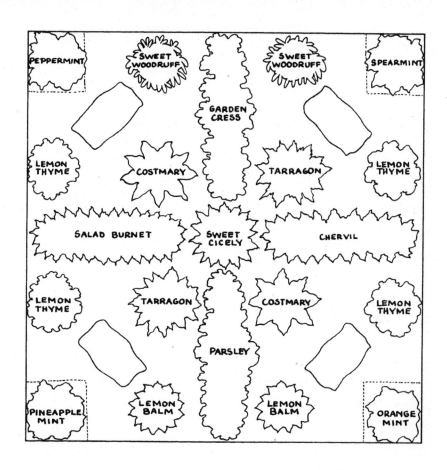

HERB	LIFE-CYCLE	AVERAGE HEIGHT	PROPAGATION METHOD
MINTS:			
orange mint	P	24"	4
peppermint	P	24"	4
pineapple mint	P	12"	4
*spearmint	P	18"	4
*tarragon	P	18" to 24"	4
lemon thyme	P	6"	4
sweet cicely	P	3'	4
sweet woodruff	P	6"	4/5

Cottage Garden

(4' x 12')

THIS GARDEN WAS PLANTED with deliberate asymmetry in an attempt to capture the informal beauty of the traditional cottage garden. German chamomile and the African blue basil make a nice contrast with the airy foliage of the dill and bronze fennel. Calendula, marigolds, and nasturtium are cottage garden staples.

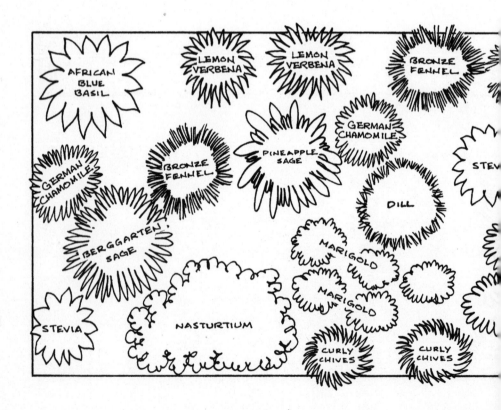

HERB	LIFE CYCLE	AVERAGE HEIGHT	PROPAGATION METHOD
African blue basil	A	30"	5
calendula	A	24"	2/3
German chamomile	a	18" to 24"	2
curly chives	P	6"	4
dill	A	30"	3
bronze fennel	A	30"	3
lemon verbena	TP	4' to 6'	5
marigold	A	8" to 18"	2
nasturtium	A	8"	3
pineapple sage	TP	30"	5
Berggarten sage	P	8" to 12"	5
stevia	TP	24"	5

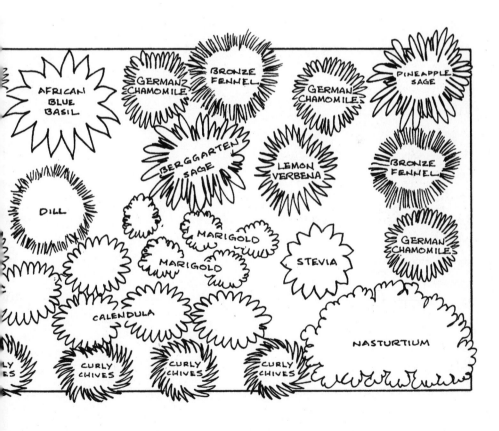

Free-Form Cottage Garden

(Approximately 4' x 8')

LIKE THE RECTANGULAR cottage garden, this garden strives for informality and a casual elegance. Stepping stones create openness and make it easier for the gardener to gain access to plants for tending and cutting. Herb plants are sometimes overlooked for their value in bouquets, but herbs such as dill, fennel, and pineapple sage add delightful accents to arrangements made with traditional cut flowers. The barbecue rosemary in this plan is in a 14" pot buried to a depth of 10". In the front border, Molly chives produce their sprightly yellow blooms in early spring. After they fade, nasturtiums can be planted in their place to provide summer color.

HERB	LIFE CYCLE	AVERAGE HEIGHT	PROPAGATION METHOD
African blue basil	A	30"	5
calendula	A	24"	2/3
German chamomile	A	18"	2
curly chives	P	12"	2/4
Molly chives	P	12"	3
dill	A	30"	3
bronze fennel	A	30"	3
dwarf marigold	A	8"	2
nasturtium	A	8"	3
pineapple sage	TP	30"	5
rosemary Barbecue	P	24"	5
stevia	TP	24"	5
English Wedgewood thyme	P	8"	5

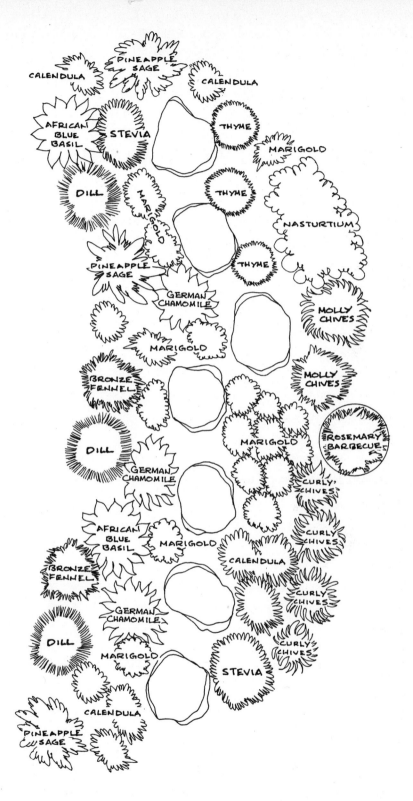

Free-Form Cottage Garden

Container Herb Gardens

HERE ARE A FEW IDEAS for growing herbs in containers. Even gardeners with plenty of outdoor space for gardens may want to adapt one or more of these plans in order to have the beauty and convenience of herbs at hand on a balcony, patio, or terrace.

Kitchen Garden

(24" to 30" half barrel)

Aussie Sweetie Basil, Berggarten Sage, Parsley Comune, English Wedgewood Thyme, Oregano Hot and Spicy, Prostrate Rosemary

Asian Garden

(24" to 30" half barrel)

Coriander, Lemongrass, Lime Basil, Saltwort, Thai Basil, Vietnamese Coriander

BBQ Bucket

(24" to 30" half barrel)

Rosemary Barbecue, Berggarten Sage, Parsley Comune, Golden Lemon Thyme, Stevia, Winter Savory

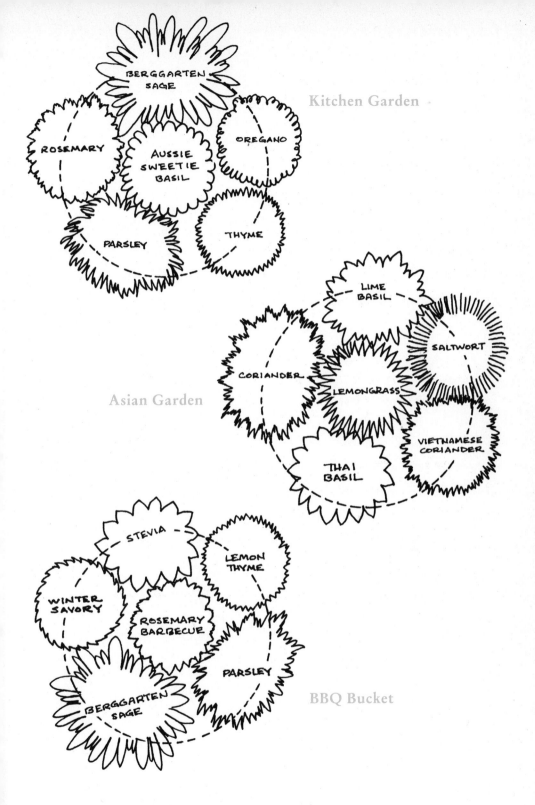

BERGGARTEN
SAGE

ROSEMARY

AUSSIE
SWEETIE
BASIL

OREGANO

PARSLEY

THYME

LIME
BASIL

CORIANDER

SALTWORT

LEMONGRASS

THAI
BASIL

VIETNAMESE
CORIANDER

STEVIA

LEMON
THYME

WINTER
SAVORY

ROSEMARY
BARBECUE

PARSLEY

BERGGARTEN
SAGE

Window Box Garden

(12" by 36" box, 10" deep)

Berggarten Sage, Chives, Winter Savory, Dwarf Basil, Golden Lemon Thyme, Oregano Hot and Spicy, Parsley Comune, Prostrate Rosemary

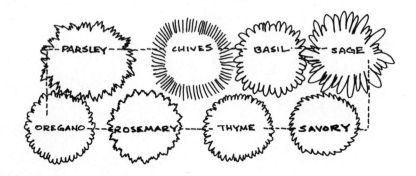

Trough Garden for the Patio or Atop Stone Wall

(24" by 72", 10" deep)

Berggarten Sage, Parsley Comune, Chives, English Wedgewood Thyme, Fernleaf Dill, Genovese Basil, Golden Lemon Thyme, Greek Oregano, Hardy Sweet Marjoram, Vietnamese Coriander, Winter Savory

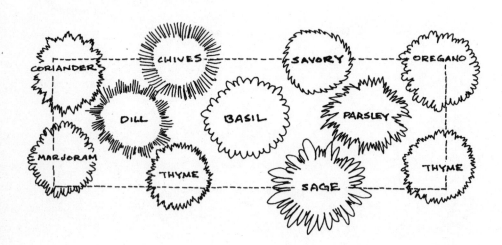

Two-Tier Garden

(24" to 30" half barrel with 12" top tier container)

Aussie Sweetie Basil, Berggarten Sage, Parsley Comune, Coriander, Creeping Winter Savory, English Wedgwood Thyme, Golden Lemon Thyme, Hardy Sweet Marjoram, Prostrate Rosemary, Oregano

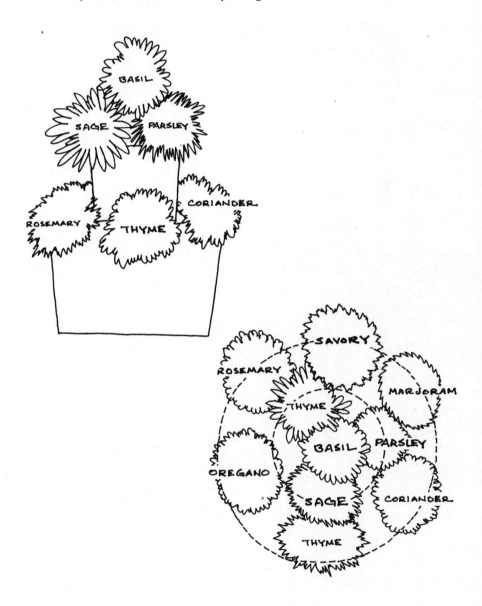

IV.
Herb Culture Guide

How to Use the
Culture Guide

HERBS MENTIONED IN THIS BOOK and used in the garden plans are indexed here alphabetically by popular name, along with details on the propagation and cultural techniques that may be particular to each plant.

The line of "vital statistics" for each herb is similar to that used throughout the plans section. It consists of these elements:

Popular Name:	For example, Ambrosia
Life Cycle:	A
Average Height:	18"
Propagation Method:	2/3
Botanical Name:	*Chenopodium*

Key:

First element: **popular name** of herb (an asterisk * appears if the herb is one of the basic fifteen culinary herbs.)

Second element: **life cycle**

A	annual
B	biennial
P	perennial
TP	tender perennial

Note: if life cycle code is bracketed—[A], [P], or [TP]—the herb described may be brought in from the garden and kept as a houseplant in a sunny window during the winter.

Third element: **average height** of plant at maturity under normal growing conditions.

Fourth element: **propagation method** suggested for each herb according to the five methods discussed in the main text.

Group 1	Cluster sowing indoors
Group 2	Spot sowing indoors
Group 3	Cluster/row sowing outdoors
Group 4	Making root divisions
Group 5	Taking stem cuttings

The **bulb method** of propagation is also included to cover some plants. As mentioned earlier, the methods recommended are not necessarily the only ways to propagate the herbs in question. But generally they are the easiest or most practical, considering such factors as seed germination rate or availability of existing plants.

Fifth element: the official **Latin or botanical name** for each herb. Whenever possible, these names conform to Bailey's *Hortus Third* (Macmillan, 1976), a respected source of horticultural data for growers, botanists, and other plant scientists, compiled by L. H. Bailey Hortorium, Cornell University. A more recent reference work is the Royal Horticultural Society's *New Encyclopedia of Plants and Flowers.*

Certain families of herbs, such as lavenders, mints, and thymes, are grouped together for convenience and comparison purposes.

ALLIUMS

Chives*

P · 12" · 1 · *Allium schoenoprasum*

Native to the Orient, chives were found in European herb gardens by the sixteenth century. Chopped or diced, the slender, hollow stems' delicate onion flavor complements almost any vegetable. They can also be mixed with cream cheese or butter. The edible rose-purple flowers can be tossed in salads, used as garnishes, or steeped in vinegar to make rose-colored chive vinegar. Chives are practically impervious to garden pests and actually repel some insects. Grow in decorative clumps at the corners of the garden. By the third growing season, chives can be dug up, divided, and set elsewhere in the garden, or given away to gardening friends.

Curly/Curled Chives

P • 6" • 4 • *Allium senescens* Glaucum

Shortest and slowest spreader of all the chive family. Produces blue-green, twisty foliage with striking lavender blossoms in July. Seeds are almost impossible to find, so buy established plants or divide a neighbor's cluster in the spring. Does better in soil that has been well-limed. Milder flavor than common chives.

Garlic Chives; also called Broad-Leaved Chives, Chinese Leeks

P • 12" • 2/4 • *Allium tuberosum*

Try planting in rows around the vegetable garden to deter pests. Lovely white blossoms appear in July. Dig up and divide every other fall. Chop the flat leaves to add garlic/chive flavor to salads or sautés, or steep the white blooms in vinegar.

Molly Chives

P • 12" • Bulb • *Allium moly*

Plant tiny bulbs in fall, 3" deep at 6" intervals. Produces bright yellow blooms in late May, which add a festive touch to spring salads.

Roseum Chives

P • 15" • Bulb • *Allium rosea*

Plant same as MOLLY. Produces rose-colored blossoms, slightly larger than its cousin, in early June; also tasty in salads.

Globemaster Allium

P · 32" to 40" · Bulb

One of showiest of ornamental onions, it is topped by 8" globes of deep violet flowers in May and early June. Hardy bulbs keep multiplying over time.

Garlic

P · 24" · Bulb · *Allium sativum*

This flat-leaved onion, a general health tonic prescribed for numerous ailments, comes in two basic types. Softneck garlic is the kind that can be braided into bunches. It is the garlic of choice among commercial growers, because it is easier to harvest by machine. Hardneck garlic is a specialty of many organic growers. It forms a woody stem and develops edible green shoots in June called scapes, which can be harvested for use in salads and stir-fries. There are many varieties within the hardneck family—German, Spanish, Italian, red, white, and so on—but the essential garlic flavor is a constant. A third garlic, called Elephant for its large cloves, is actually more closely related to leeks and is very mild in flavor. Plant cloves in fall to a depth of 4" to 6" at 6" intervals. Harvest in midsummer after leaves have dried and died down. Save some for replanting in fall for next year's crop.

Leeks

P · 24" · 1 · *Allium ampeloprasum*

Start indoors from seed about 60 days before setting out in the garden; separate seedlings and transplant 6" to 8" apart. Milder in flavor than ONIONS, leeks can be hilled with soil as they develop to blanch the base.

Onions

B · 18" · Bulb · *Allium cepa*

Depending on variety selected, may be started from seed, seedlings, or sets (tiny bulbs). Sets are simpler and quicker. If sowing from seed, be sure to thin seedlings to 6" apart. Prefers sweet, moderately rich soil. Harvest in fall after stalks have turned brown and fallen over. Southport onions, from our neighboring town of Southport, Connecticut, have enjoyed a resurgence of popularity in recent years and their seed is readily available from heirloom seed sources.

Egyptian Onions

P · **12"** · **Bulb** · *Allium cepa proliforum*

Plant bulbs in fall. Tiny new bulblets develop in clusters on top of tall hollow stems, which are often crooked. Use some of the bulblets to perpetuate the crop every fall. Mild flavor enhances eggs, salads, soups, and sauces.

Shallots

P · **15"** · **Bulb** · *Allium cepa var. aggregatum*

Plant from bulbs in fall (with mulch to protect from frost) or very early spring. Bulbs multiply into clumps, which should be harvested after foliage dies down in late summer or early fall. Replant small bulbs each year. Mild flavor esteemed in Mediterranean cooking.

Welsh Onions

P · **18"** · **3/4** · *Allium fistulosum*

Start from divisions in fall, or sow the seed of this variety of bunching onions in the spring. In fall harvest as needed, separating smaller bulbs from clumps to replant for new crop. Will self-sow. Young shoots can be harvested and used like CHIVES.

ALOE VERA

[TP] · **12" to 24"** · **4** · *Aloe barbadensis*

Spiky, gray-green succulent leaves with skin-healing properties used to treat sunburn, kitchen burns, rashes, and minor cuts. Tolerates light shade; must be brought indoors in pots in northern areas.

AMBROSIA; also called JERUSALEM OAK

18" · **2/3** · *Chenopodium botrys*

Easily started from seed. Self-sows every year, but not so prolifically as to become a nuisance.

ANGELICA

B • 6' • 3 • *Angelica archangelica*

Seeds must be really fresh to germinate, so I don't recommend buying them in the spring. Instead, locate fresh seed in fall and sow immediately outdoors. Seedlings will emerge, then die down to the ground after freezing, and reappear the next spring as strong healthy plants. Unlike most herbs, this large grower likes a rich soil. It also does better with shade half the day. Will self-sow.

ANISE

A • 24" • 3 • *Pimpinella anisum*

Easily started from seed, but doesn't like being transplanted because of tap root. Sow at shallow depth in spot you want plants to grow. Mound plants as they develop, as stems tend to be weak. Both seed and leaves have licorice flavor. Harvest flower clusters when seeds turn brown.

ARTEMISIAS

Mugwort

P • 3' • 2/4 • *Artemisia vulgaris*

Ancient magical plant and the only perennial artemisia, besides wormwood, for which seeds are readily available. Very hardy, rapid grower, producing dark green leaves with white, downy undersides; keep confined by dividing after second year.

Roman Wormwood

P • 18" • 4 • *Artemisia pontica vulgaris*

Divide every other year to prevent overly heavy growth. Prone to fungus problems in damp weather.

Silver King

P • 24" to 36" • 4 • *Artemisia ludoviciana* var.

Cultivate regularly to keep fungus from forming at base of plant. Spreads rapidly, so subdivide in early spring every other year after second growing season. Popular in dried arrangements and herb wreaths.

Silver Mound

P • 6" • 4 • *Artemisia schmidtiana* Nana

Develops into a stunning solid mound-shaped mass of lacy, silvery leaves, especially in hot and dry growing conditions. Shaped as it is, little air circulation reaches base of plant, so it is extremely susceptible to rot during wet weather. If this happens, cut back to the ground and plant will revive, though it may not reestablish its attractive form in the same season.

Silver Queen

P • 24" • 4 • *Artemisia* var.

Slightly broader leaves than SILVER KING and tends to grow shorter and showier. Requires same care as other artemisias.

Southernwood; also called Old Man

P • 3' • 4 • *Artemisia abrotanum*

Easily started from divisions in early spring. Finely cut, aromatic gray foliage gives plant a delicate, airy appearance. Sprigs and branches can be harvested twice during growing season for use in bouquets and dried arrangements. Erect grower, keeps good shape. Subdivide every spring after second year. Used dried in clothes closets to repel moths.

Wormwood

P • 24" • 2/4 • *Artemisia absinthium*

Bitter herb used to make the long-banned liqueur absinthe. Transplants well after being started from seed even though it has a large and fast-growing tap root. Subdivide every other year. Like SOUTHERNWOOD, an effective moth deterrent.

ARUGULA
See ROQUETTE

BALM
See BEE BALM, LEMON BALM

BASIL*; also called BUSH BASIL, SWEET BASIL

A ・ 18" ・ 2 ・ *Ocimum basilicum*

Sweet basil has a bushy growing habit with profuse leaves of such fragrance when fresh that the plant is known as "the royal herb" in France. Its flavor has been described as rich and peppery, with nuances of clove and mint. Basil is a mainstay in Italian cooking, renowned for making pesto and flavoring fish and vegetables, especially tomatoes, peppers, eggplant, and beans. This most tender culinary herb should not be set in the garden until warm temperatures are the norm. Today, it has eclipsed virtually all herbs in popularity, and as a result, numerous varieties have been developed, offering different flavors, colors, leaf sizes, and growth patterns.

African Blue Basil

A ・ 30" ・ 5 ・ *Ocimum basilicum* var.

A distinctive, decorative plant with an attractive purplish-blue cast, strong growth habit, and sweet camphor scent. Reproduce from cuttings.

Aussie Sweetie Basil; also called Greek Columnar

[A] ・ 36" ・ 5 ・ *Ocimum basilicum* var.

This relatively new basil variety has a tall, slender profile and dark green leaves with strong basil flavor; performs well indoors in areas with cold winters. Does not produce seeds, so must by propagated by cuttings.

Cinnamon Basil

A · **18" to 24"** · **2** · *Ocimum basilicum* **var.**

Native to India, this herb combines the traditional clove flavor of basil with cinnamon for a unique, spicy taste welcome in many recipes in Indian and Asian cuisine.

Dwarf Basil

A · **12"** · **2** · *Ocimum minimum* **Spicy Globe**

Shortest of basils. Has small leaves, but seeds true to form are hard to find. Dense globular bush will maintain shape throughout growing season, so an excellent choice for pots or other containers. Keep picking off flowers.

Fine-Leaf Basil

A · **15"** · **2** · *Ocimum basilicum feinum*

Good border plant. Medium-sized leaf and plant, very popular with French chefs.

Genovese Basil

A · **12" to 30"** · **2** · *Ocimum basilicum* **Genovese**

Deep green, very shiny leaves, which curl slightly, intense perfumed flavor, and vigorous growth. Do not plant outside until nighttime temperatures stay above 50°F. Water consistently, pinch flowers, and make pesto! Many new varieties of this subspecies have been developed in recent years, ranging in height from 12" to 30".

Lemon Basil Sweet Dani

A · **18"** · **2** · *Ocimum americanum*

High in essential oil and citrus flavor, this basil has small, pale green leaves and a delightful lemony fragrance useful in potpourris, teas, and as a traditional seasoning in pea soup.

Lemon Basil

A · 18" · 2 · *Ocimum basilicum x citriodora*

Excellent lemon scent with large, dark green leaves, pink flowers, and robust growing habit.

Lime Basil

A · 16" · 2 · *Ocimum americana* var.

The bright green leaves of this compact plant, giving off a clean lime scent, are highly desirable for making potpourri and in Thai cooking.

Thai Siam Queen Basil

A · 18" to 24" · 2 · *Ocimum basilicum* var.

A regal-looking plant with small green leaves and purple stems and flowers; its spicy anise-licorice aroma and flavor are cherished in Thai and Vietnamese cuisine.

Lettuce-Leaf Basil

A · 18" to 24" · 2 · *Ocimum basilicum crispum*

Largest leaves of all the basils; seed readily available. Needs plenty of room in the garden.

Basil Nufar

A · 24" · 2 · *Ocimum basilicum* var.

Genovese variety rich in aroma and flavor and the first sweet basil resistant to the disease fusarium wilt.

Basil Osmin Purple; also called Dark Opal Basil

A · 18" · 2 · *Ocimum basilicum* var.

Best of the purple basils. Deep iridescent purple leaves with fuchsia blossoms glow in the garden. Full basil aroma and flavor turns white vinegar a deep burgundy color. Cross-pollination with other basils will develop seed that produces plants streaked with green, so make sure of the reliability of your seed source for this one.

Sacred Basil; also called Holy Basil

A · 30" · 2 · *Ocimum basilicum sanctum*

One of the largest of all the basils. Should be hilled or staked. Seeds hard to come by. Pungent, fruity aroma retained in dried leaves for years. Venerated in Hindu religion.

Basil—Sal's Italian Choice

A · 24" · 2 · *Ocimum basilicum* Genovese

Developed from Franchi Sementi seed from Italy, variety features dark green, slightly curled foliage, great flavor, strong growth habit, and excellent leaf production.

BAY*

[TP] · 2' to 6' · 5 · *Laurus nobilis*

Indigenous to the Mediterranean area and Asia Minor, this evergreen tree grows naturally to a height of 40', but in much smaller sizes must be transplanted to containers and moved indoors in northern climates. Its leaves formed the ancient laurel wreath used to crown scholars and poets, and garlands of it were awarded to the champions at the first Olympic Games in 776 B.C. A mainstay of French and Italian cuisine, bay's distinctive flavor is released when leaves are added to slow-cooked soups, stews, and sauces. Beans, rice, lentils, and other grains also benefit from the inclusion of bay in their preparation.

BEDSTRAW

See LADY'S BEDSTRAW

BEE BALM; also called BERGAMOT, OSWEGO TEA

P · 30" · 4 · *Monarda didyma* varieties

Start from division in early spring as soon as new growth appears. If you wait until it reaches 8", you'll risk losing the plant in the process of dividing. Erect grower and rapid spreader, as member of mint family; it should be divided yearly after second season as root systems become highly developed. Most impressive in mass plantings. Scarlet, lavender, pink, and white varieties also available. Susceptible to mildew, so allow plenty of light and air circulation, and do not overwater.

BORAGE

A · 30" · 2 · *Borago officinalis*

Simple to start from seed—if seed is fresh. Germination rate is practically 100 percent. Likes a richer soil than most herbs. Supposed to self-sow, too, although I've never seen it happen in any of my gardens. (We have a problem growing borage in our greenhouses because for some reason mice collect the seed from our sowing trays and bury the seed elsewhere, where clumps of borage inconveniently sprout days later.) Blue or white flowers, depending on variety, and hairy leaves. So-called "herb of gladness" is used in teas; chopped young leaves add cucumber tang to salads and lemonade.

BURNET; also called SALAD BURNET

P · 18" · 2 · *Proterium sanguisorba*

For constant supply of cucumber-flavored greens, keep cutting young leaves when 4" to 5" high. A low grower suitable for edgings and borders. Divide after second growing season. First perennial salad herb ready to harvest in early spring.

CALENDULA; also called POT MARIGOLD

A · 24" · 2/3 · *Calendula officinalis*

Germinates in 10 days at 65°F. If started indoors, use peat pots. If outdoors in the garden, keep picking the flowers and you'll see new blooms all summer long. Petals give delicate flavor and strong color to salads and omelets. A valued ingredient in herbal skin creams and hair rinses.

CHAMOMILE; also called GERMAN CHAMOMILE

A · 18" to 24" · 2 · *Matricaria recutita*

Easily started from seed but does not transplant well unless plant is strongly developed. Sow in peat pots. Keep picking flowers for your teas before seed ripens or it will self-sow all over the garden. In the Beatrix Potter tale, the apple-flavored tea made from this chamomile was served to Peter Rabbit.

Dyer's Chamomile; also called Yellow Chamomile, Golden Marguerite

P · 30" · 2 · *Anthemis tinctoria*

Largest of all the chamomiles, produces a bright yellow daisy-type flower. Germinates easily, but seeds are harder to obtain than other chamomiles. Divide after second growing season. Useful as cut flower and to make natural yellow and golden dye.

Roman Chamomile; also called English Chamomile

P · 6" · 1 · *Chamaemelun nobile*

A terrific groundcover that will take all kinds of abuse and still come back. Does not bloom nearly as profusely as the tea chamomile (German chamomile), but its flowers can also be used to brew tea.

CARAWAY

B · 24" · 2 · *Carum carvi*

Very hardy biennial that can be harvested for its seed early in second year. Young carrot-like seedlings do not transplant well, so start in peat pots, which can be transplanted intact into garden. Sow outdoors (Group 3 method) in early fall to get crop of seed toward end of the next growing season. Adds its distinctive flavor to cabbage dishes, rye bread, buns, and cakes.

CATNIP

P · 18" · 2/3 · *Nepeta cataria*

Easily grown indoors from its tiny seeds; germinates in 4 days. Outdoor sowing must await warmer soil. Divide after second season. Can be cut to ground several times in season. Self-sows readily, so keep it from going to seed unless you have a lot of cats to support.

Catnip Mussinii

P • 12" • 4 • *Nepeta mussinii*

Much smaller than common catnip, with attractive silver-blue foliage. Not as delectable to cats, but excellent in dried bouquets. Hard to find the seed, so make a division in a friend's garden in early spring. Divide after second or third year. With so many useful traits as a landscape perennial, this variety has been developed into several hybrid forms.

CAYENNE PEPPER

A • 30" • 2 • *Capsicum annuum*

Like all other peppers, this is relatively easy to grow from seed, but don't overwater young seedlings that are started indoors as they easily dampen off. Transplant into garden after all danger of frost is past. Needs moderately rich soil. If you let a fruit or two fall to the ground during the growing season, the plant may self-sow.

CHERVIL*

A • 16" • 2 • *Anthriscus cerefolium*

Chervil is most widely known in French cooking; its anise-tarragon flavor makes it a desirable substitute for parsley and a must ingredient in béarnaise sauce and French vinaigrette. Chervil combines particularly well with eggs, vegetables, and salads. In cooking, always add chervil at the end for best flavor. Its fern-like leaf structure is as delicate as its flavor is subtle. It prefers a cool season and goes to seed quickly in summer heat. Use as fresh as possible, as leaves lose their mild taste rapidly in drying. Chervil, along with parsley, thyme, and tarragon, are the famous *fines herbes* of French cooking—the four horsemen of the culinary apocalypse.

COMFREY

P • 36" • 4 • *Symphytum officinale*

Easily started from root divisions in early spring. Extremely hardy, will spread rapidly in any sunny location. Divide yearly to keep it confined. Useful as green manure crop, animal fodder, and compost builder.

CORIANDER/CILANTRO*

A • **24"** • **2** • *Coriandrum sativum*

Coriander gets its name from *koris,* the Greek word for bedbug. This less than glamorous association is explained by the herb's unusual fragrance, a combination of sage and citrus flavors that some people find unpleasant. Indeed, it is one of the "bitter herbs" brought to the table by Jewish families at Passover. Yet its leaves and seeds are highly valued in many of the world's cuisines, including Mexican, Thai, and Indian. A tall, slender annual with bright green leaves, it thrives in poor soil and, like thyme, is a magnet for bees. It goes to seed quickly in summer, so sow fresh seed every 3 weeks for a constant crop.

Coriander/Cilantro Delfino

A • **18"** • **2** • *Coriandrum sativum* **Delfino**

Slow to bolt, this variety from the Netherlands has fern-like foliage that sets it apart from other cilantros. Very aromatic and highly recommended for containers and small gardens.

Vietnamese Coriander/Cilantro

A • **4"** • **5** • *Polygonum odoratum*

Not a coriander, botanically, but has desirable cilantro flavor and fragrance. Its cascading growth habit makes it suitable for hanging baskets. Does not produce seed. Keep picking leaves and stems for bushier growth.

CORN SALAD; also called MACHE

A • **8"** • **3** • *Valerianella locusta*

Bolt-resistant salad green with mild nutty flavor. Grows quickly from seed if soil is warm. Ready in 45 days; sow for spring and fall harvests.

COSTMARY; also called BIBLE LEAF

P • **36"** • **4** • *Chrysanthemum balsamita*

Seeds hard to locate, but divides easily in early spring. Will grow well in shade, but will not blossom unless in sun. Divide after second growing season, as it becomes too large and straggly. Leaves have sweet mint-balsam fragrance. Nickname comes from use as bookmark and insect deterrent in family Bibles in earlier times. Versatile herb—can be used in teas, potpourris, and salads.

CRESS; also called GARDEN CRESS

A · 6" · 3/4 · *Lepidium sativum*

A piquant salad herb not to be confused with WATERCRESS. Grows quickly from seed; does better in moderately rich soil. Make several sowings during summer. The Upland Cress variety has the neatest, most compact growing pattern.

WATERCRESS

B · 3" · 1 · *Nasturtium officinale*

Start indoors in peat pots. Seeds sprout in 2 weeks; thereafter, growth is rapid. Plant in shallow brook of fresh, unpolluted water in spots protected from full force of running water—buffer with stones if necessary. If you have a so-called overflowing well, you can use the extra runoff as your seed bed for this cress. Begin harvest within 2 to 3 weeks and keep harvesting until water source runs dry. May self-sow for following year.

CURRY

[TP] · 15" · 5 · *Helichrysum angustifolium*

Not to be confused with curry powder, which is a combination of several ground spices. Can be started only from cuttings. Can be brought indoors in winter; its silver foliage makes it an attractive houseplant. Not supposed to be winter-hardy, but it has survived four straight winters in our Connecticut gardens. Leaves have a strong, sweet curry scent, but not recommended in cooking because of bitter taste.

DANDELION

P · 4" · 3 · *Taraxacum officinale*

Simple to start from seed sown sparingly. Keep picking flowers to promote growth of the leaves for use in salads. Valued in Europe for its nutritional properties.

DILL*

A · 30" · 3 · *Anethum graveolens*

This tall, feathery herb held a place of honor in the gardens of ancient Greece and Rome. If planted in rich, well-drained soil in a hot, sunny spot in the garden, dill will self-sow readily, but for a continuous summer harvest, sow fresh seeds in rows every 3 weeks. Dill is delicious with eggs, cucumbers, potatoes, and many kinds of fish, especially salmon. Seeds have a stronger flavor than foliage and are used whole or ground in longer-cooking recipes.

Dill Bouquet

A · 24" · 3 · *Anethum graveolens* var.

This variety is somewhat more desirable in gardens than standard dill because of its short, compact growing pattern. Resows itself readily, so is often called a perennial. Seeds used in pickling recipes; leaves in sour cream, cucumber salads, and egg and cheese dishes.

Dill Fernleaf

A · 15" · 3 · *Anethum graveolens* var.

Seeds are extremely expensive—about twenty times the cost of other dill seed—but many gardeners prefer this variety for its neat growing habit and attractive, dark green foliage.

DITTANY OF CRETE

[A] · 10" · 5 · *Origanum dictamnus*

Easy to start from cuttings unless over-watered. Its root system does better bound in a small pot. Will survive as a houseplant if trimmed and brought indoors in a clay pot to a sunny window in winter months. Replant in garden in following spring. No oregano flavor, but in southern gardens will produce an attractive mauve-pink flower suitable for dried arrangements.

DYER'S BROOM

P • 18" • 2 • *Genista tinctoria*

Divide after second growing season. If allowed to go to seed, will self-sow freely. A great dye plant with a strong yellow color.

ELECAMPANE

P • 4' • 4 • *Inula helenium*

Seeds are hard to find and hard to germinate, so start from division of a friend's established plant in early spring. Because of its height and broad leaves, this plant requires more moisture than most herbs do. Its stately profile makes it a good choice for a background plant. Primarily for medicinal use.

EPAZOTE

A • 24" to 30" • 3 • *Chenopodium ambrosioides*

Strong, weedy growing habit; petroleum-like scent of its leaves makes it a popular ingredient in Mexican and Caribbean recipes, especially black bean dishes, quesadillas, and moles.

EUCALYPTUS

[TP] • 6' • 2 • *Eucalyptus globlus*

A tree that grows to 100 feet in its native habitat, this makes an excellent tub plant up north if you can keep it in a sunny window indoors in the winter. Needs a moderately rich soil. Other varieties: HEART-SHAPED, SPIRAL, APPLE, HONEY, LEMON, PEPPERMINT.

FENNEL

A • 30" • 3 • *Foeniculum vulgare*

Grown exactly like dill, this herb has leaves and seeds with a sweet anise flavor particularly tasty in fish and pork dishes. The seeds are also used in Swedish limpa rye bread. A tender perennial variety, BRONZE FENNEL

RUBRUM has metallic dark brown foliage and is grown primarily for its decorative value, but it too has an anise flavor that can be used in salads and oily fish courses. A prolific self-sower.

FEVERFEW White Stars

P • 24" • 1 • *Chrysanthemum parthenium*

Robust plant with fragrant foliage and daisy-like flowers, which when dried are said to repel moths. Once thought to reduce fevers and cure headaches, and even today is the focus of research related to migraine pain. Keep picking blossoms and stems and it will continue to flower all summer.

FOXGLOVE

B • 36" • 2/1 • *Digitalis purpurea*

Seeds are slow to germinate. Beware of over-watering young seedlings. Transplant to a rich, well-drained soil. Full sun is essential for development of the digitalis content in leaves. Flowers in spectacular fashion in second year. (If started indoors in December or January, it will flower in the first year.) Hybrid varieties can reach 6' in height.

GARDEN CRESS

See CRESS.

GERANIUMS

See SCENTED GERANIUMS.

GINSENG

P • 16" • 2/4 • *Panax quinquefolium*

Very hard to grow from seed. Buy established 3-year-old roots instead. Needs a well-drained, rich, loamy soil in a cool, shady spot, preferably in a wooded area. Considered one of the most important medicinal herbs, it takes several years for the root to grow large enough for harvest.

GOLDENSEAL

P · 12" · 2/4 · *Hydrastis canadensis*

Grown like ginseng, but its roots develop more quickly and are ready for use in medicinal applications in 2 years.

GOOD KING HENRY

P · 8" · 3 · *Chenopodium bonus henricus*

A pleasant, mild-tasting pot herb prepared like spinach. Seeds are difficult to find, so let some of your plants go to seed for use in the following season.

HELIOTROPE

[A] · 18" · 5/2 · *Heliotropium arborescens*

Peruvian native with purple, vanilla-scented blooms. Relatively easy to start from seed indoors, but a better growth pattern develops when cuttings are made from choice plants. Prefers moderately rich soil. Will survive as a houseplant if trimmed and brought indoors in a clay pot to a sunny window in winter.

HOPS

P · 6' to 8' · 4 · *Humulus lupulus*

A well-known flavoring for beer, this energetic vine with its pinecone-like blossoms is ideal for growing on trellises and arbors. Many varieties available.

HOREHOUND

P · 18" · 2 · *Marrubium vulgare*

Easily started from seed; germinates in 10 days at 70°F, 20 days at 55°F. Will grow in partial shade, but prefers full sun. Will rot away in wet locations. Though hardy, will not survive a wet winter. Divide after second growing season.

HORSERADISH

P · 24" · 4 · *Armoracia lapathifolia rusticana lupulus*

Start from root or piece thereof in very early spring for a good fall crop the following year. Grows tenaciously in any kind of soil in a sunny location. Grate for a pungent relish or condiment with meat or fish. Named Herb of the Year in 2011.

HYSSOP

P · 24" · 2 · *Hyssopus officinalis* var.

All the flowering hyssops of this species—red, pink, and white—are easy to grow from seed, and if the seed is fresh, you'll get 90 percent germination. Prefers a well-limed soil and will do fairly well in partial shade. Natural deterrent of white fly in gardens and greenhouses. Old plants become woody, so replace with fresh plants when they become unattractive.

JERUSALEM ARTICHOKE

P · 7' · 4 · *Helianthus tuberosus*

Grown primarily for the sweet, nut-like flavor of its potato-shaped tubers. Start from tubers in early spring. Grows quite tall and produces a mass of flowers that resemble small sunflowers in late fall.

KOREAN MINT

P · 30" · 2 · *Agastache rugosa*

Interesting but little-known tea herb, best started from seed simply because it may be hard to find plants from which to make a division. Will grow up to 4' tall the second year in rich soil. Oriental variety of anise hyssop, *Agastache foeniculum*, with sweet, anise-like scent and flavor.

LADY'S BEDSTRAW; also called YELLOW BEDSTRAW

P · 24" · 2 · *Galium verum*

Seeds germinate slowly and not very well, but once established in the garden, the plants spread well and should be divided every spring beginning with the third growing season. Does well in partial shade.

LADY'S MANTLE

P · 12" · 4 · *Alchemilla vulgaris*

Sprays of delicate, chartreuse-colored flowers are long-lasting, freshly cut or dried. Best way to propagate is by division in early spring, but requires more careful handling than most perennials because of its deep tap roots. If allowed to go to seed, it will sometimes resow itself in early fall; transplant these seedlings to a cold frame for distribution to friends and neighbors next spring. Susceptible to rot unless in a well-drained spot.

LAMB'S EARS; also called BETONY

P · 12" · 4 · *Stachys byzantina; vulgaris*

Soft, downy foliage with rose-colored flower spikes. Divide in early spring and give it plenty of room. To keep it from overcrowding itself, redivide every second year.

LAVENDERS

All lavenders are hard to start from seed indoors; propagate via cuttings to get more uniform and compact growth from new plants. Take a deep breath and trim plants the first year to keep them from flowering and so promote bushier growth—and a prolific harvest the next year. Thereafter, trim every year after flowers have been harvested. Lavenders have long tap roots, so they are not easily transplanted after 2 years.

Lavender Fred Boutin

P · 12" to 15" · 5 · *Lavandula x intermedia*

Vigorous growing, highly fragrant variety with silvery gray foliage and lavender blue flowers on 24" stems. Blooms in late spring and early summer.

Lavender Goodwin Creek

TP · 12" to 15" · 5 · *Lavandula dentate*

Dense hybrid variety developed by Jim and Dolly Becker of Oregon blooms on and off throughout summer. Softly scalloped leaf edges and deep purple flowers.

Lavender Grosso

P • **15" to 18"** • **5** • *Lavandula x intermedia* **Grosso**

Developed as an important commercial strain in the Vaucluse region of France, this variety has a strong scent and violet flowers on very long stems that add another 24" to 30" to height of plant. Likes a high pH of 7 to 7.5, so incorporate lots of lime in area where it is grown.

Lavender Munstead; also called English Lavender

P • **15"** • **2/5** • *Lavandula angustifolia* **Munstead**

Earliest-blooming English lavender, with smallest leaves and compact growth habit; named for Gertrude Jekyll's famous perennial garden.

Lavender Provence

P • **12" to 15"** • **5** • *Lavandula x intermedia*

A hybrid with rich, sweet scent and large plant size with deep violet blooms on long stems. Requires sweet soil (pH 7.8).

Lavender Spike

TP • **18" to 24"** • **2/5** • *Lavandula spica*

Tallest but least hardy lavender, with broad gray leaves and a hint of camphor in its scent.

Lavender Vera

P • **18"** • **2/5** • *Lavandula angustifolia* **var.**

Best choice for most gardeners, this English lavender variety grows as a shrub with narrow, aromatic gray leaves, and lavender blooms on spikes.

LEMON BALM

P • **18"** • **4/2** • *Melissa officinalis*

Easily started from division or seed in early spring. Does well in full sun or semi-shade. Harvest several times—leaves are most flavorful before flowering. Divide every year after second year, as it spreads quickly. Do not let them go to seed or the garden will become overcrowded with them.

LEMONGRASS

TP • **36"** • **2** • *Cymbopogon flexuosus*

Native to Sri Lanka and India, plant forms dense, tall clumps of broad grass blades that smell intensely of lemon drops. (An Asian variety, CITRATES, has a fennel-like base and is propagated only by division.)

LEMON VERBENA

[TP] • **6'** • **5** • *Aloysia triphylla*

Has the truest lemon scent of all the lemon-flavored herbs, so is extremely popular ingredient in beverages and potpourris. Needs rich soil and lots of sun and warmth. Start from cuttings if you can't buy established plants, but be patient, as it is one of the hardest herbs to propagate. As a houseplant over winter, needs a tub-sized planter and sunny window. Goes into semidormancy until February, then starts to produce new leafy growth. Victorians floated its leaves in finger bowls.

LICORICE

[A] • **12"** • **5** • *Helichrysum petiolatum*

A decorative herb, not the true licorice plant, with attractive silver-gray foliage that makes for an excellent houseplant in pots or hanging baskets.

LOVAGE

P • **6'** • **2** • *Levisticum officinalis*

Start from seed indoors about 6 weeks before you intend to set it out in the garden—no earlier, or its rapid growth will need more space. Requires richer soil and more moisture than most herbs because of its size. Will tolerate partial shade. Divide every other year in early spring unless you happen to have plenty of room for it in the garden. Leaves taste of celery with a curry overtone and are recommended as a salt substitute. Use in salads and soups and to add meaty richness to vegetarian dishes.

MADDER

P · 12" · 4 · *Rubica tinctorum*

Seeds are hard to obtain, so find a friend with madder and make a division in early spring—there'll be plenty of underground runners to pick from. Divide every year after second growing season to keep confined. Roots are used for making red dye.

MARIGOLDS

A · 15" · 2 · *Tagetes spp.*

Probably the easiest of all annual herbs to start from seed. Thanks to extensive hybridization, now comes in more sizes than poodles. Shorter ones work best in small areas, though. Some varieties produce edible lemon-flavored flowers that can be used as garnishes in salads.

MARJORAM

Sweet Marjoram*

TP · 12" · 1 · *Origanum majoricum*

A symbol of marital harmony (fashioned into crowns, the herb was placed on the heads of Greek newlyweds), sweet marjoram tastes a bit like a mild oregano with a hint of balsam. A staple in French and Italian cuisine, it in fact can be substituted for oregano on pizza and in eggplant Parmesan and lasagna dishes. Harvest leaves just as blooms begin; flowers resemble small green knots. Use pungent leaves to rub roasts, or add to soups during last 15 minutes of cooking.

Wild Marjoram

P · 18" · 1 · *Origanum vulgare*

Hardier than its sweet cousin but bland in scent and flavor. Often mistakenly sold as oregano. Divide after second growing season to keep confined. Self-sows profusely if allowed to drop seed. Pink-purple flowers attract bees.

MEXICAN TARRAGON; also called MEXICAN MINT MARIGOLD

P • 14" to 18" • 2/5 • *Tagetes lucida*

Sweet-smelling leaves make an excellent substitute in warm areas where French tarragon will not grow. Golden yellow, marigold-like flowers. Makes a stimulating tea.

MINTS

Dozens of varieties of this tenacious grower offer a wide range of flavors for enhancing many different beverages and foods. Most mints thrive in partly shady locations that receive plenty of moisture. Their rampant growth can be contained by sinking barriers around each planting to a depth of 12" to 16". Greek, Middle Eastern, and Indian cooking all make extensive use of the mint family in recipes.

Spearmint*

P • 18" • 4 • *Mentha x spicata*

Spearmint is a favorite for adding to fruit salads and all kinds of meat, fish, and vegetable dishes. Like many of the mints, it can also be used for brewing tea, hot or iced.

Apple Mint

P • 24" • 4 • *Mentha suaveolens*

Grows taller than the other mints but less profusely, with larger, woollier leaves with a distinct apple-camphor fragrance.

Black Peppermint; also called Black English Peppermint, Brandy Mint

P • 15" • 4/5 • *Mentha x piperita* **var.**

This variety has very dark leaves and stems with excellent peppermint flavor; its pungency deters insects. Mexican and other Spanish cultures use this herb extensively in cooking and for its soothing properties when used for tea.

Crisped Scotch Mint

P • 14" to 18" • 4 • *Mentha x gracillis spicata* **Crispa**

An easily grown mint that spreads quickly, crisped Scotch mint has smooth, rounded green leaves with a strong scent.

Curly Mint

P • 18" • 4 • *Mentha x spicata* **var.**

Almost exactly like spearmint but very crinkly; its true mint taste suits teas and fruit and green salads.

Golden Ginger Mint

P • 14" • 4 • *Mentha x spicata* **var.**

Another variation on spearmint, with smooth dark leaves with splashes of chartreuse along the veins.

Orange Mint

[P] • 24" • 4 • *Mentha x piperita*

True orange tang makes it a favorite for teas, jellies and salads. Known as the "eau de cologne" mint, it has broad, dark green leaves.

Pennyroyal Mint

P • 3" • 3 • *Mentha x pulegium*

Short and small-leaved, but strongly flavored and a natural flea deterrent. Unlike most mints, this one is easy to start from seed.

White Peppermint

[P] • 24" • 4 • *Mentha piperita*

Second most popular of all the mints after spearmint; has darker stem and smaller leaf. The strong, heady taste of this peppermint makes it the mint of choice for making chewing gum, candy, and other sweets.

Pineapple Mint

P · 12" · 4 · *Mentha suaveolens* Variegata

Attractive variegated leaf. Much smaller than its first cousin, apple mint. When propagating, pick most desirable color variation in leaf.

MITSUBA; also called JAPANESE PARSLEY

P · 8" to 10" · 2 · *Cryptotaenia japonica*

Easy-to-grow, vigorous plant, prefers more moisture and less sun than most herbs. Leaves and stems are used as parsley in Japanese dishes.

MOTHERWORT

P · 30" · 2 · *Leonurus cardiaca*

Easy and quick from seed. Control by dividing regularly after second growing season.

MULLEIN

B · 4' to 6' · 2 · *Verbascum phoenicum*

Easily started from the tiny seeds if they are fresh—germinates in 10 days at 70°F—and transplanted into garden when young, but sets down deep tap root so is hard to move after second year. Needs very dry, poor soil to do well; fertilize and it practically shrinks. Produces huge velvety gray-green leaves, called donkey ears, at the base of its large yellow flower spike. Cut the flower before seed ripens and drops, or you will have thousands of seedlings springing up in your garden next year.

MUSTARD

A · 18" · 3 · *Brassica sinapis*

Germinates in 30 hours at 70°F—that's fast. For plenty of tender young leaves, sow succession crops of this cabbage relative for use in salads and as cooked greens. Seeds are ground to make the condiment mustard.

NASTURTIUMS

A • 8" • 3 • *Tropaeolum majus*

Easily started from seed outdoors, but make sure soil is warm. Available in an array of gorgeous colors. The edible leaves and flowers add spice and brightness to salads.

NETTLE

P • 36" • 3 • *Urtica dioica*

The herb least loved by my workers in the greenhouses. Easy to start from seed, but hard to transplant because even as a seedling it has stinging spines. Keep dividing after second year in garden to confine growth.

OREGANO*

P • 24" • 4 • *Origanum* var.

The hot, peppery flavor of this herb makes it a desirable ingredient in many Italian recipes for pasta, meats, and tomato sauces. It also enhances egg and cheese dishes, including frittatas, omelets, and quiches, and combines well with olive oil, garlic, parsley, and thyme. Before buying established plants, take a bite of a leaf to be sure you are getting a variety with kick. Varieties such as Mexican, Greek, and Syrian oreganos are often spicier than so-called "true" oregano.

Greek Oregano

P • 12" to 24" • 2/4 • *Origanum vulgare hirtum*

A very spicy oregano, the strongest of all, this herb comes in various shapes and sizes, as its seed is collected in the wild in Greece; excellent seasoning with meats, tomato dishes, and sauces.

Oregano Hot and Spicy

P • 8" • 4 • *Origanum vulgare*

Compact, dense grower with rich deep green leaves and (often) red stems; its fiery edge spices up any meal.

Mexican Oregano

TP · 24 to 30" · 5 · *Lippia graveolens*

This variety has a fine oregano flavor used to great advantage in chilis and other Mexican dishes. When properly pruned, it will grow into a miniature tree in a bright window or solarium.

Syrian Oregano—Sal's Choice

[P] · 24" to 30" · 5 · *Origanum maru*

Large, gray-green leaves on straight stems deliver consistently strong oregano flavor. This variety from Syria, sometimes called Maru, is tallest of the oreganos, but does not spread so is easy to control in the garden. Extremely hardy.

ORANGE OSAGE

[P] · 6' · 2 · *Maclura pomifera*

Grows to forty feet in Texas and Arkansas, and makes a good tub plant up north if you have the room inside the house. A poor germinator, so sow plenty of seed to ensure obtaining a seedling or two.

PARSLEY*

B · 8" · 3 · *Petroselinum neopolitanum*

Flat leaf parsley, also called Italian parsley, has more flavor than curly parsley and is an important ingredient in dishes around the world, including tabbouleh in the Middle East, persillade in France, tempura batter in Japan, and parsley butter in England. It combines well with other herbs in many recipes. Its high chlorophyll content also makes it a natural breath sweetener. It likes full sun and an evenly moist rich soil. A row of six to eight plants will keep the cook in the family well supplied with this versatile herb. As a biennial, it goes to seed quickly in the spring of its second year in the garden.

PARSLEY COMUNE

B · 18" · 3 · *Petroselinum* Comune

Flavorful flat leaf parsley variety is used in cooking throughout Italy; frost-resistant, dark green foliage, and a vigorous growth habit.

PERILLA Britton; also called SHISO

A · **18" to 30"** · **3** · *Perilla frutescens*

Spicy Asian herb with green leaves and red undersides; mild mint-basil flavor enhances salads and sushi. Green and purple leaf varieties have lemony cinnamon tang. Self-sows readily.

POPPY

A · **24" to 36"** · **2** · *Papaver rhoeas*

Not to be confused with opium poppy (*Papaver somniferum*), a perennial that is illegal to grow in this country. Annual varieties produce more seed than perennials, and so are more desirable in most herb gardens. Poppies are available in numerous colors and need more nourishment and moisture than the typical herb.

PYRETHRUM

P · **18"** · **2** · *Chrysanthemum cineraiifolium rhoeas*

Slow grower in first year; showy, daisy-like flowers appear in second year. Divide in spring of third year. Source of pyrethrins—organic insecticide used to combat flies, mosquitoes, and other insects.

RED VALERIAN; also called FOX'S BRUSH, RED COW BASIL

P · **36"** · **4** · *Centranthus rubber*

Often confused with valerian (garden heliotrope) because of the name, but it's a different plant. Compact grower, easily started from division. Flowers profusely in August. Young leaves can be eaten in salads and cooked as greens.

ROQUETTE; also called ROCKET or ARUGULA

A · **10"** · **3** · *Eruca vesicaria sativa*

Quick and easy from seed. Harvest leaves when young and tender; if allowed to flower, leaves become tough and bitter. Resow several times during season.

ROSEMARY*

[TP] • **12" to 24"** • **5** • *Rosmarinus officinalis*

Rosemary is a tender perennial shrub with green needle-like leaves and pale blue flowers. Its pungent aroma has been described as a combination of pine and mint with an undertone of ginger. Once an important medicinal herb, it has many applications in today's kitchens. It is a frequent complement to roast chicken, fish, lamb, veal, beef, pork, and game, and enhances tomatoes, peas, squash, spinach, and other vegetables. Bring indoors to a cool, sunny location and you can harvest leaves throughout the winter months.

Rosemary Barbecue

[TP] • **36"** • **5** • *Rosmarinus officinalis* **var.**

Dark green variety with a strong, erect growing habit; stems can be used as skewers for grilling meat and vegetables.

Rosemary Foresteri

[TP] • **4'** • **5** • *Rosmarinus officinalis*

Strong growth pattern with broader, heavier leaves and stems than *R. officinalis* has. This variety is also known as Lockwood de Forest.

Pine-Scented Rosemary

[TP] • **18"** • **5** • *Rosmarinus officianalis angustifolia*

Compact grower with short leaves and stems; thin leaf pattern. One of most manageable rosemary varieties to have indoors. Has strong pine fragrance and can be trained into miniature "Christmas tree" topiary for the holidays if you start pruning the plant in August.

Prostrate Rosemary

[TP] • **6"** • **5** • *Rosmarinus officinalis* **Prostratus**

Excellent creeping plant for borders or rock gardens, but does best in full sun. Bring inside, in a hanging basket to enjoy its profusion of tiny blue blossoms in winter. "I lett it runne all over my garden wall," wrote St. Thomas

More, "not onlie because my bees love it, but because 'tis the herb sacred to remembrance, and therefore to friendship."

Rosemary Sal's Choice

[TP] · **24" to 30"** · **5** · *Rosmarinus officianalis* **var.**

Vigorous grower with upright stems and deep green foliage. Developed in Israel, this variety has great flavor; one of best rosemary varieties on the market.

White-Flowering Rosemary

[TP] · **24"** · **5** · *Rosmarinus officianalis* **Albus**

Strong-flavored sprigs with rare white flowers, recommended for pork and lamb roasts. Not as susceptible as other rosemarys to powdery mildew indoors during winter months.

RUE

P · **24"** · **2** · *Ruta graveolens*

This "herb of grace" germinates quickly from seed—in 5 to 7 days at 70°F. Transplants easily. Pinch off flower stalks as they appear and plant will stay more attractive and compact. Replace with new plant after third year to keep it from taking over area. Some people are allergic to rue, especially in hot weather; bare skin that touches rue leaves may develop a rash.

SAFFRON; also called TRUE SAFFRON

P · **8"** · **Bulb** *Crocus sativus*

Takes 3 years to get flowers from seed, so buy bulbs in late summer or early fall. Plant 4" apart, pointy ends up (like garlic cloves). Lavender flowers with bright orange stigma appear in 4 to 5 weeks, and every fall thereafter. Dried stigma are used for color and flavor—it takes 60,000 stigma to produce 1 pound of saffron.

SAFFLOWER; also called FALSE SAFFRON, DYER'S THISTLE

A • 24" • 2 • *Carthamus tinctorius*

Grown primarily as an oil seed crop, its large oval seeds sprout quickly and easily, but seedlings become floppy if started too early indoors. Make sowing 4 weeks before date of setting out into garden. One of most attractive yellow/orange flowering herbs, blossoms resemble SAFFRON. (Another seed, like BORAGE, inexplicably coveted by mice in the greenhouse.)

SAGE*; also called GRAY SAGE, COMMON SAGE, GARDEN SAGE

P • 24" • 3 • *Salvia officinalis*

Another Mediterranean native, sage grows as a hardy shrub with wiry, woody stems bearing velvety, grayish-green leaves with a pleasantly bitter lemon-camphor flavor. The herb's culinary value goes well beyond use as an ingredient in stuffing for the annual Thanksgiving turkey. Young sage leaves can be sprinkled in salads and cooked in omelets, fritters, sausages, and meat pies. Sage also goes well with a multitude of vegetables. Common garden sage can grow into a good-sized shrub, but other culinary varieties will remain more compact. Sage produces pink, purple, blue, or white flowers. With its numerous varieties and low maintenance requirements, it is always a welcome addition in herb gardens or flower borders. An ancient Arabic saying alludes to the herb's medicinal properties: "How can a man die whilst sage grows in his garden?"

Berggarten Sage*

P • 8" to 12" • 5 • *Salvia officinalis* Berggarten

A lovely compact bush with large, rounded, silvery leaves and lilac-blue flowers; strong sage flavor. A nice addition to a garden where space is limited. Mildew-resistant.

Clary Sage

B · 4' · 2 · *Salvia sclarea*

One of the tallest sages, has large silvery, fuzzy leaves; rosy blue or white flowers appear in second year. Self-sows readily if flowers are allowed to mature and drop seed. If started in garden in late summer, will flower following year.

Dwarf Gray Sage

[TP] · 8" · 5 · *Salvia officinalis* Dwarf

Miniature version of the basic culinary sage; useful in confined areas and patio planters. Best sage to pick for winter houseplant—manageably small and has desired flavor.

Golden-Edged Sage

P · 15" · 5 · *Salvia officinalis* Aurea

Yellow-and-gray variegated leaf makes this compact grower a decorative border element.

Nazareth Sage

P · 14" to 18" · 5 · *Salvia lavendulifolia*

A hybrid form of common garden sage, this is a compact grower suitable for container plantings. Leaves are elongated and silvery gray; pale purple flowers. Can be used fresh or dried for its full sage flavor.

Pineapple Sage

TP · 36" · 5 · *Salvia elegans*

Must be treated as annual in northern climate, but well worth the trouble for its splendid red flowers and fragrant pineapple aroma. Growth is stunted in cool springs, but will shoot up once warm weather begins. Use to garnish fruit salad, iced tea, and fruit juice drinks.

Purple Sage

P ▪ 15" ▪ 5 ▪ *Salvia officinalis* **Purpurea**

Stunning dark purple foliage and compact growth habit makes this herb a graceful addition to mixed borders as well as herb gardens.

Tricolor Sage; also called Silver Edge Sage

P ▪ 15" ▪ 5 ▪ *Salvia officinalis* **Tricolor**

Medium-sized hardy plant produces attractive leaves of cream, purple, and green with good sage flavor. Makes a great accent plant in any garden.

ST. JOHN'S WORT

P ▪ 18" ▪ 3 ▪ *Hypericum perforatum*

Keep confined by spading out perimeter growth in the fall and harvesting flowers. If allowed to self-sow, it will spread like a weed.

SALAD BURNET

See BURNET.

SALTWORT; also called JAPANESE SEAWEED

A ▪ 8" ▪ 1 ▪ *Salsola komarovii*

Succulent, crunchy leaves of this traditional Japanese herb are added to salads and sushi or steamed for a nutritious side dish.

GRAY SANTOLINA; also called LAVENDER COTTON

P ▪ 12" ▪ 5 ▪ *Santolina chamaecyparissus*

Best grower of all the santolinas, can be trimmed or shaped into an attractive hedge or border. If untrimmed, produces pretty, small yellow flowers that look good in dried bouquets. Becomes overly woody and should be replaced after 4 to 5 years. Like all santolinas, an excellent deterrent to insects.

SAVORY

Summer Savory*

A · 18" · 3 · *Satureja hortensis*

Called the bean herb in German cooking, and traditionally used with all beans from green to lentils, this hardy annual with delicate lavender flowers self-sows easily. Its leaves have a peppery, thyme-like flavor that blends well with other herbs and spices. Also a good companion for strong-flavored brassicas, such as cabbage and brussels sprouts. With its branching root system, summer savory benefits from more water than most herbs do.

Winter Savory

P · 12" · 2 · *Satureja montana*

Very slow from seed—must be started indoors at least 3 months before setting out. Compact, cascading growing habit lends itself to planting in containers. Normally hardy but will suffer winterkill in very wet conditions. May become overly woody and need replacement in 3 to 4 years. Coarse, stronger flavor than SUMMER SAVORY, excellent seasoning with beans, cabbage, and turnips.

SCENTED GERANIUMS

Cinnamon

[TP] · 18" · 5 · *Pelargonium x limoneum*

Sturdy, erect-growing plant with fine-toothed, fan-shaped leaves and small lavender flowers. Lemon scent in summer has cinnamon overtone in winter.

French Lace

[TP] · 18" · 5 · *Pelargonium crispum* Prince Rupert

Erect grower like lemon, but with crinkled, cream-bordered leaves. Weaker lemon scent. Hardest to start from cuttings.

Lemon

[A] • 24" to 30" • 5 • *Pelargonium limoneum*

Small, crinkly round leaves branch out from tall, sturdy form; can be shaped into handsome topiary if trimmed regularly.

Lime

[TP] • 18" • 5 • *Pelargonium nervosum*

Small, roundish, deep green leaves, dark lavender flowers, and astringent lime scent. Grows more slowly than LEMON.

Nutmeg

[TP] • 18" • 5 • *Pelargonium x fragrans*

Small grayish leaves, busy growing pattern. Nutmeg scent is sweet and spicy.

Peppermint

A • 24" • 5 • *Pelargonium tomentosum*

Fastest grower and spreader, with powerful peppermint aroma. Has large, velvety, silver-green leaves. Too big to bring inside intact. In typical growing season will grow two to three times the breadth of rose geranium, or about 4' across. To bring inside, start new plant from cuttings in late summer.

Rose

A • 24" • 5 • *Pelargonium graveolens*

Most popular of all scented geraniums; has deeply cut, heart-shaped leaves, spreads to 2' across, but with more erect pattern than peppermint. Start from cuttings in late summer if you want this one indoors for winter.

Snowflake

A • 24" • 5 • *Pelargonium capitatum* Snowflake

Strong, busy grower with round, deep green leaves with specks of white. To bring indoors, start new plant from cuttings in late summer. Pick sprig with most attractive color variation—what you see is what you will get.

SORREL; also called FRENCH SORREL

P · 18" · 3 · *Rumex scutatus*

Self-sows readily, so keep harvesting or it will crowd out other herbs. Early in second year, keep cutting flower stalks as they appear. Remove crop and replant from new seed in third year, otherwise it gets too high and its leaves too tough.

STEVIA

TP · 24" · 5 · *Stevia rebaudiana*

Bushy, somewhat shade-tolerant plant produces leaves said to be a hundred times sweeter than table sugar but without the calories; powdered leaves can be used to sweeten drinks, baked goods, desserts, and preserves. Harvest entire plant as flower buds appear. Difficult to grow from seed; cuttings produce stronger plants.

SWEET CICELY

P · 24" · 4 · *Myrrhis odorata*

With its anise-celery flavor, this white-flowering herb brings out the best in cabbage, parsnips, and carrots. Nearly impossible to start from seed. Likes partial shade. Develops heavy root systems that should be divided in early spring after third year. Don't confuse with the wild American sweet cicely (*Osmorhiza longistylis*), which grows freely in many northern wooded areas.

SWEET MYRTLE

[TP] · 18" · 5 · *Myrtus communis* Microphylla

Takes patience to start from cutting, but easy to grow once established. One of the herbs used by the ancient Greeks to crown poets, its tiny glossy leaves produce a pleasant, spicy scent when rubbed together. If bringing indoors as a houseplant in the fall, cut back slightly as you would for rosemary. Leaves can be used like bay in cooking.

SWEET WOODRUFF

P • 8" • 4/5 • *Asperula odorata*

Division is the best way to propagate. Nearly impossible from seed, and cuttings take well only if protected from hot sun while rooting. If starting from cutting, locate rooting medium in filtered sunlight and keep moist. The established plant likes a cool, shady, moist spot in the garden—don't let it dry out in summer drought or you'll lose it. A lovely spreading ground cover for shady areas—a bed of this herb is a sight to behold. Its white flowers and leaves make a delicious tea, but it is best known as the essential ingredient in May wine.

TANSY

P • 36" • 2/4 • *Tanacetum vulgare*

Simple to start from division in early spring, but gets too big topside to do so safely any later. Its aggressive root system needs plenty of room and occasional composting or manuring. Subdivide after second growing season and each year thereafter to keep confined. Yellow button flowers dry well; the leaves can be used to make a pale green dye.

FERN-LEAF TANSY

P • 18" • 4 • *Tanacetum vulgare crispula*

A smaller, less rapid-growing version of tansy, considered more attractive because of its fern-like leaf, though it will not produce as many flowers. Subdivide after second season and every other year thereafter.

TARRAGON*

P • 30" • 4 • *Artemisia dracunculus*

Tarragon complements chicken, fish, and egg dishes with its subtle, anise-like flavor and makes an outstanding vinegar for use in salads and marinades. It is a key ingredient in such classic preparations as remoulade sauce, French dressing, tartar sauce, and béarnaise sauce. Also use it to flavor mayonnaise, butter, sour cream, and yogurt. The species name, *dracunculus*, refers to the curling, coiling growth habit of its root system. Once a common remedy for toothaches, its leaves have a numbing effect when chewed.

TEUCRIUM GERMANDER

P · 15" · 5 · *Teucrium chamaedrys*

Easy from cuttings but takes weeks for roots to develop. Lends itself to shaping into small shiny-leaved hedges similar to boxwood, for use in border plantings and knot gardens. Very hardy, but don't trim late in season or it may lose vitality in some areas during a severe winter (as happens to boxwood).

MILK THISTLE

A · 24" to 30" · 2 · *Silybum marianum*

A striking plant with creamy white and bright green marbled leaves, which develop into sharp needles as season progresses. Heads are frequently eaten like artichokes. Extract of the herb is sold as a treatment for liver problems in mainstream drugstores and supermarkets. Some gardeners plant thistles in a border to deter critters.

THYME*; also called ENGLISH THYME, COMMON THYME

P · 12" · 1 · *Thymus vulgaris*

A little plant with a big personality, its leaves have a fresh green taste with a hint of clove. This most useful of cooking herbs grows as a small, many-branched shrub, which bees love (when it's in flower) almost as much as chefs do. A Mediterranean herb that is a staple in French cuisine, as well as Cajun and Creole cooking styles, it works well with meats, fish, shellfish, and all kinds of vegetables, and complements the flavors of basil, rosemary, garlic, and lemon. Thyme is so aromatic it is also used to make cologne, soaps, and after-shave.

Caraway Thyme

P • 1" • 4 • *Thymus herba-barona*

Low creeping variety spreads rapidly. Divide every 2 or 3 years. Foliage has a strong caraway scent and flavor that enhances vegetables, soups, poultry, and game. "Baron" in its botanical name refers to an English baron's favorite roast, flavored with the thyme.

Creeping Scarlet Thyme

P • 1" to 3" • 4 • *Thymus serpyllum splendens*

Similar to white except grows taller, less compactly. Has darker foliage and fuchsia-colored blossoms.

White-Flowering Thyme

P • 1" • 4 • *Thymus praecox* Albus

Lowest-growing thyme, has light green foliage, grows thickly, and spreads quickly. Tiny white flowers appear in June. A good variety for filling in between flagstones or bricks in walkways.

Dwarf Winter Thyme; also called German Thyme

P • 12" • 1 • *Thymus vulgaris* var.

Treat exactly as English Thyme. More compact growing habit.

English Wedgewood Thyme

P • 8" • 5 • *Thymus vulgaris* Wedgewood

A hybrid variety of COMMON THYME has variegated chartreuse green foliage with light lavender flowers. Makes an eye-catching accent plant in the herb garden and does not get as woody as COMMON THYME.

French Thyme

P • 12" • 1 • *Thymus vulgaris* var.

Narrower, more delicate leaves than ENGLISH THYME and a slightly stronger flavor. Needs winter protection; may not be hardy in northern gardens. The thyme of choice for French chefs.

Golden Lemon Thyme

[P] · **8"** · **5** · *Thymus aureus x citriodorus*

A slow spreader, started from cuttings; select for best variegation and color. Makes good pot plant if brought indoors to a cool, sunny window. Often used to shape into bonsai plants. Stems develop a red hue in coolness of early spring. Intense lemon flavor lends itself to use with fruit, iced tea, broiled or grilled fish, and poultry.

Lemon Thyme

P · **6"** · **4** · *Thymus citriodorus*

Rapid spreader needs division every 2 or 3 years. Glossy, dark green leaves have strong lemony flavor, but will lose scent if cross-pollinated with other varieties, so keep flowers trimmed. One of best natural insect repellents in the garden or on the patio.

Orange Balsam Thyme

P · **6" to 12"** · **5** · *Thymus* **Orange Balsam**

Green-gray foliage and pale pink flowers; has a very pungent citrus-thyme scent and flavor; used in fruit salads and vinegars.

Oregano Thyme

P · **8"** · **5** · *Thymus* **var.**

A small evergreen shrub with shiny, bright green leaves, larger than those of other thymes. Spreads slowly, so not easy to start from division. Often preferred as oregano substitute in Italian cuisine.

Pink Thyme

P · **1" to 3"** · **4** · *Thymus serpyllum roseus*

Exactly like CREEPING SCARLET THYME except for color of blossoms.

Silver Lemon Thyme

[P] · 8" · 5 · *Thymus x citriodorus* **Argenteus**

Shrub-like thyme with striking gray and cream foliage; strong lemon thyme scent and flavor.

Woolly Thyme

P · 1" · 4 · *Thymus pseudo-lanuginosus*

Fuzzy, blue-gray foliage, rapid spreader, and easily divided, but most prone to rot of all the thymes, so do not plant where taller plants will shade it, and do not mulch for winter. Ideal for cascading over walls and rocks, or as a border, spilling out onto pathways. Loves a hot, sunny location.

VALERIAN; also called GARDEN HELIOTROPE, PERENNIAL HELIOTROPE

P · 3' to 4' · 4 · *Valeriana officinalis*

Will flower at end of first season, every August thereafter. Pink, lavender, or white blooms have a sweet fragrance that attracts cats. Subdivide after the second growing season and every other year thereafter. Benefits from annual manuring or composting. Because it self-sows readily, it's designated an invasive plant in some states, including Connecticut (an ill-considered ruling, in my opinion; we have had it in our medicinal herb display garden for more than 30 years and have not had an invasiveness problem).

VERVAIN

P · 24" · 2 · *Verbena officinalis*

Bushy grower. Pick off its small purplish flowers or it will self-sow widely. Divide every other year.

VIOLETS

P · 4" · 3/4 · *Viola odorata*

Fragrant small flowers in wide range of colors; performs well in partial shade and rock gardens; prefers fairly rich soil. Subdivide every third year or plants will become too crowded.

WOAD

B · 36" · 3 · *Isatis tinctoria*

Does not flower until second year; harvest blossoms promptly to prevent fierce self-sowing. Traditionally used to dye wool and fabrics blue.

YARROW

P · 24" · 2/4 · *Achillea filipendulina*

Seeds available but hard to get to sprout. Still, if interested in specific color—red, pink, salmon, yellow, or white—it's sometimes better to go by the seed than by guesses about what color flowers your neighbor's yarrow will produce. Needs a bit more moisture than average herbs. Divide after second growing season and every other year thereafter.

Harvesting & Storing
the 15 Basic Herbs

INFORMATION SUPPLIED HERE is limited primarily to special harvesting and storing techniques for each of the fifteen basic culinary herbs. These are applicable to many of the herbs featured in the other garden plans, too.

There are five simple ways to save the goodness of a summer's crop of herbs: My favorite method is to lay fresh herbs between layers of paper towels to absorb any excess moisture, and keep them out of the light to retain their natural color and essential oils. Or, bundle the herbs in bunches and hang them in a dark, dry location, such as a closet or cupboard, or in paper bags. Another method is to spread herbs on baking sheets and place in the oven set at low heat, bearing in mind that different herbs dry at different rates. Pack herbs in convenient portions in plastic storage bags, and place in the freezer. Or save herbs in bottles filled with white vinegar.

For more detailed, plant-specific instructions:

Basil

Cut sprigs or leaves as needed, beginning 4 weeks after date of transplant. Pinch out flowering tops whenever they appear.

For saving: Freeze in recipe-sized portions, or hang to dry in small bunches in a dark place. Basil darkens readily in too much heat, so be extra careful if oven-drying. For large-leaf varieties, strip leaves from stems and lay between layers of paper towels. Once dried, crumble them with your fingers or pass them through a coarse sieve before storing in jars.

To preserve basil in vinegar, introduce several fresh sprigs into a wide-mouthed bottle filled with white vinegar and let stand away from the light for 2 or 3 weeks. You end up with two products for off-season use—basil-flavored vinegar and the basil leaves themselves, which can be extracted, rinsed, and used as fresh. The dark opal variety turns the vinegar a pleasant rose pink or lavender color.

Remember to make your final harvest of basil before the first 40°F night, or you may lose this very tender plant.

Bay

In first year, pick out central stem about 1" to make the plant bush out, then harvest sparingly, selecting leaves around the base of the plant so as to allow this slow grower to develop properly.

For saving: We suggest bringing your bay plant inside in its pot for the winter. If you do that, you don't have to worry about storing the harvest. However, bay is easily dried for winter use, too. Spread leaves between layers of paper towels or in a single layer on a tray and leave in a warm dark room for 1 or 2 weeks, with a board or book on top of the leaves to keep them from curling.

Chervil

Cut the lacy leaves as needed 8 weeks from sowing of seed. Cut from the outside of the plant so it keeps growing up and out from the center.

For saving: A lot of cooks say chervil is not worth drying because its small leaves get even smaller in the process and its delicate flavor is practically negligible in the dry state.

But see what you think. Harvest before flowering, place in thin layers on paper towels, or dry on trays in a good spot or in your oven, then store in jars in a pantry or cabinet.

Chives

Take small bunches from each plant rather than giving a crew-cut to one plant at a time. Cut it down to 1" and the plant will come back several times in the season. Also, you'll see more attractive purple flowers per clump around June.

For saving: Harvest as above, but get rid of the yellow and tough shoots, then chop into 2" lengths and spread on a tray or screen and dry quickly in an oven at a very low heat.

Some people think you get more flavor freezing chives than you do drying them. In preparation for freezing, wash the chives, pat them dry, and eliminate poor-looking ones. Then chop and store in plastic bags in the freezer.

Coriander/Cilantro

If you're growing primarily for its leaves (sold as Chinese parsley or cilantro in Oriental or Spanish markets), harvest as needed, beginning 8 weeks from sowing date.

If you're growing it for the seeds, then let plants mature, harvesting leaves sparingly if you wish. In late summer, harvest seed heads after the first seeds have turned brown. Then place between layers of paper towels, or hang seed heads upside down in your drying spot and let the rest of the seed ripen. Place a clean tray or similar container immediately beneath the bunch to catch the seed as it falls—if the seed falls from a greater height, it will bounce all over the place. That's why some people prefer to catch it in paper bags. Anyway, store the collected seed as is—don't crush or grind it.

Dill

The foliage can be lightly harvested throughout the growing season, beginning 6 weeks after plants first appear. Don't cut too deeply, though, or you'll hamper development of the umbels, or seed heads. Best leaf flavor is at the time of flowering.

For saving: The seed heads should be cut after the first seeds have turned brown, just as with coriander. Hang them upside down in a good spot and let the seed drop onto a tray or into a bag as it matures. Or dry it in a slow oven before saving.

Use the seed to make dill vinegar, or store in airtight jars in a dark place. The dried seed will keep its flavor for several years.

The foliage on dill plants can be saved, too. During growing season, after taking seed heads and before foliage turns brown, harvest, wash, pat dry, and store the leaves in plastic bags in the freezer. Or dry them in bunches and then strip the leaves for storage. Or chop them first and dry on paper towels.

If a few seed heads do mature on the plant and fall to the ground, they might survive under a winter mulch and show up as volunteers the following spring.

Oregano

Cut sprigs and leaves in about 4 to 6 weeks, or as soon as a good growth pattern has been established. In the first year, this would be about when the plant has reached 6" in height and 6" across. In succeeding years, wait until plant has produced 4" to 6" in new growth, in the spring.

For saving: Harvest within 4" of the ground every month, and hang in bunches in a dry, dark place. Some gardeners prefer to wait until flowers appear before harvesting, but don't get as much foliage harvest if they do.

Parsley

In the first year, begin cutting 8 to 10 weeks after sowing date. Harvest as needed, cutting to within 1" to 2" from ground level to ensure four to six harvests per season.

In the second year, begin cutting immediately as soon as new growth appears, as this biennial will go to seed quickly. Don't count on more than one harvest.

For saving: Cut the plants down by half at midsummer. Take final harvest after the first light frost in fall.

Some cooks think frozen parsley has a better flavor than dried parsley. Wash sprigs, pat dry, chop off stems, and then freeze in freezer bags. Don't thaw before using, as it will come out limp.

To dry, hang in small bunches, place between paper towels, or process in a slow oven. Then crush it or put it through a coarse sieve before storing.

Rosemary

Harvest sprigs as needed. Don't cut into the woody parts that develop after the second year or you could hinder the plant's development.

For saving: Dry sprigs on a tray or screen—the leaves will look like pine needles when finished. Strip off the leaves and store.

Sage

Once the plant begins to grow vigorously in the garden, cut leaves and sprigs as needed. In the first year this may not be until midsummer. In succeeding years you can begin the harvest just as soon as new tender growth appears on the bush.

For saving: Cut 6" to 8" top growth two to four times per year, after the first year.

Sage can be dried in small bunches or in thin layers. Its tougher leaf usually requires a bit more time for adequate drying than any of the other basic herbs.

Spearmint

Cut sprigs and leaves as needed. This is one herb you don't have to be fussy about in harvesting, even in its first years in your garden. It will grow no matter how you treat it.

For saving: Harvest at the onset of flowering—you should be able to get many harvests in one season.

Always handle mint with care—like tarragon, its leaves bruise easily.

Hang in small bunches or lay out in thin layers and dry in slow oven, then strip leaves and store in jars.

Spearmint can be crushed before storing, but peppermint—the mint preferred for teas—is better left in leaf form and used that way in making infusions (see Tea Garden notes in the Plans section).

Summer Savory

Make the first picking of tender new shoots about 8 weeks after plants first appear, or when they are 4" to 6" high. Then they'll begin to grow vigorously, and within 4 to 5 weeks you should be able to harvest regularly as needed. It's a much more prolific grower than its hardier cousin, winter savory, and under average conditions you should be able to harvest from it every other week throughout the growing season if you don't cut it too far back at any one time.

For saving: Cut leafy tops before buds appear. Leaves get noticeably darker after blossoming and are not as attractive to dry and store. Hang in small bunches or dry on paper towels or trays, then strip leaves for storage.

Marjoram

Harvest leaves and sprigs as needed in the first year, beginning 4 to 6 weeks after transplant into the garden. After the first year, you can make a good picking of marjoram, as of summer savory and oregano, nearly every other week in the growing season. Make your final harvest after the first frost.

For saving: Cut, wash, bunch-dry on paper towels in a good spot, or oven-dry with care. Strip free of stems and store.

Tarragon

Cut fresh leaves as needed beginning about 6 to 8 weeks after transplant into the garden in the first year—this herb takes a bit longer to get established than the other perennials. Once it has a good growth pattern, when it is about 6" to 8" across, you can harvest selectively. After the first year, cut to within 2" of the ground as needed every month in the growing season.

For saving: Handle tarragon leaves carefully; like mint leaves, they bruise easily and lose their aroma. Dry in bunches or on trays. For vinegar, cut four or five stems and immerse in a bottle of white vinegar, then cap and store for a couple of weeks in a cool dark area, such as a cupboard or cabinet.

Thyme

In the first year, cut sprigs beginning 6 weeks from date of transplant, but don't harvest too intensively or too deeply. In succeeding years you can take more of it and more often, but avoid cutting into woody stems. Make a final cut after the first frost.

For saving: Cut 6" of leafy tops before flowers actually appear. It's easy to dry thyme on trays or screens, because it doesn't hold that much moisture to begin with. When it becomes brittle, strip the leaves of the stems, then store.

Start from Scratch Schedule

THIS SCHEDULE FOR STARTING A BASIC culinary garden is based on an average date of last frost in the spring of *May 10* and an average date of first frost in the fall of *October 10*. Gardeners in areas of the country with different frost dates can adapt the schedule simply by determining their own frost dates and working from there.

Group 1 ✦ Cluster Sowing Indoors

	Chives	Marjoram	Thyme
sow seed	Feb. 15	Feb. 15	Feb. 15
at 70°F seed germinates in	5 days	7 days	5 days
Move to cooler place (50°–60°F)	March 1 to 5	March 1 to 15	March 1 to 15
pinch out tops	—	April 1	April 1 to 15
transplant to garden	April 20	May 1	April 20
begin to harvest	June 1	June 1	June 1

Group 2 ✦ Spot Sowing Indoors

	Basil	Chervil	Coriander
sow seed	March 30	March 15	March 15
at 70°F seed germinates in	7 days	7 days	5 days
Move to cooler place (50°–60°F)	May 1	April 15	April 15
pinch out tops	May 15	—	—
transplant to garden	May 25	May 10	May 10
begin to harvest	June 15	June 1	June 15

Group 3 ✦ Cluster Sowing Outdoors

	Dill	Parsley	Summer Savory
set out containers to warm soil	May 10	May 1	May 10
sow seed	May 15	May 5	May 15
seed germinates in	5–7 days	10–15 days	5–7 days
remove plastic covers	June 1	June 1	June 1
remove containers	June 10	June 10	June 10
pinch tops	—	—	June 10
begin to harvest	July 1	July 1	July 1

Group 4 ✦ Making Divisions of Spreading Perrenials

	Mint	Oregano	Tarragon
make division and plant	April 15	April 15	April 15
pinch tops	May 15	May 15	May 15
begin to harvest	June 15	June 15	June 15

Group 5 ✦ Taking Cuttings of Single-Stem Perennials

	Bay	Rosemary	Sage
make cutting	Dec. 1–Jan. 1	Feb. 1	Feb. 1
at 70°F roots form in	6–8 weeks	3–4 weeks	3–4 weeks
transplant into pots	March 15	March 15	March 15
pinch tops	June 1 or 6" high	April 1	April 1
transplant to garden	June 1	May 10	May 10
begin to harvest	late summer	mid-July	mid-July
bring in for winter	Oct. 30	Oct. 30	—

Sources

U.S. Cooperative Extension Service

The Cooperative Extension Service is a nationwide educational network. Each state and territory has an office at its land-grant university and a network of local and regional offices. These offices are staffed by experts who provide practical and research-based information for farmers and gardeners, small business owners, youth groups, and consumers in rural areas and communities of all sizes. County agents are also listed under "Cooperative Extension Service" in the phone book. To access Cooperative Extension Service systems online, by state and/or county, go to www.csrees.usda.gov/Extension.

Seed and Plant Sources

This is a representative list (in alphabetical order by state) of firms in the U.S. and Canada that do business via mail order and furnish herb, vegetable, and flower seed catalogs to home gardeners on request. Most seed and plant dealers now list their products online; in fact, some companies have discontinued print catalogs altogether. Make sure that at least some of the seeds and plants you order originate with companies in your region of the country, so that you have a choice of varieties that have been developed to thrive in the climate conditions of that region.

Native Seeds/SEARCH
526 N. 4th Ave.
Tucson, AZ 85705
www.nativeseeds.org

Terroir Seeds/Underwood Gardens
P.O. Box 4995
Chino Valley, AZ 86323
www.underwoodgardens.com

J. L. Hudson, Seedsman
P.O. Box 337
La Honda, CA 94020
www.jlhudsonseeds.com

Mountain Valley Growers
38325 Pepperweed Rd.
Squaw Valley, CA 93675
www.mountainvalleygrowers.com

Natural Gardening Co.
P.O. Box 750776
Petaluma, CA 94975
www.naturalgardening.com

Peaceful Valley Farm & Garden Supply
P.O. Box 2209
Grass Valley, CA 95945
www.groworganic.com

Redwood City Seed Co.
P.O. Box 361
Redwood City, CA 94064
userwebs.batnet.com/rwc-seed

Renee's Garden
6116 Highway 9
Felton, CA 95018
www.reneesgarden.com

The Kitazawa Seed Co.
P.O. Box 13220
Oakland, CA 94661
www.kitazawaseed.com

Chas. C. Hart Seed Co.
P.O. Box 9169
Wethersfield, CT 06109
www.hartseed.com

Comstock, Ferre & Co.
263 Main St.
Wethersfield, CT 06109
comstockferre.com

Gilbertie's Herb Gardens
7 Sylvan Ln.
Westport CT 06880
www.gilbertiesherbs.com

Kitchen Garden Seeds
23 Tulip Dr.
Bantam, CT 06750
www.kitchengardenseeds.com

New England Seed Co.
3580 Main St., Bldg. #10
Hartford, CT 06120
www.neseed.com

Shepherd's Garden Seeds
30 Irene St.
Torrington, CT 06790
www.shepherdseeds.com

Eden Organic Nursery Services
P.O. Box 4604
Hallandale, FL 33008
www.eonseed.com

The Gourmet Gardener
12287 117th Dr.
Live Oak, FL 33008
www.gourmetgardener.com

Vaughn Seed Co.
5300 Katrine Ave.
Downers Grove, IL 60515

Gurney's Seed & Nursery Co.
P.O. Box 4178
Greendale, IN 47025
www.gurneys.com

Henry Field Seed & Nursery Co.
P.O. Box 397
Aurora, IN 47001
www.henryfields.com

Earl May Seed & Nursery
208 N. Elm St.
Shenandoah, IA 51603
www.earlmay.com

Seed Savers Exchange
3094 N. Winn Rd.
Decorah, IA 52101
www.seedsavers.org

Skyfire Garden Seeds
1313 23rd Rd.
Kanopolis, KS 67454
www.skyfiregardenseeds.com

Ferry-Morse Seed Co.
601 Stephen Beale Dr.
Fulton, KY 42041
www.ferry-morse.com

Fedco Seeds
P.O. Box 520
Waterville, ME 04903
www.fedcoseeds.com

Johnny's Selected Seeds
955 Benton Ave.
Winslow, ME 04901
www.johnnyseeds.com

Farmer Seed & Nursery
818 NW 4th St.
Faribault, MN 55021
www.farmerseed.com

Seeds of Change
P.O. Box 152
Spicer, MN 56288
www.seedsofchange.com

Baker Creek Heirloom Seeds
2278 Baker Creek Rd.
Mansfield, MO 65704
www.rareseeds.com

Thompson & Morgan
220 Faraday Ave.
Jackson, NJ 08527
www.tmseeds.com

Harris Seeds
355 Paul Rd.
Rochester, NY 14624
www.harrisseeds.com

Stokes Seeds
P.O. Box 548
Buffalo, NY 14240
www.stokesseeds.com

Abundant Life Seeds
P.O. Box 279
Cottage Grove, OR 97424
www.abundantlifeseeds.com

Nichols Garden Nursery
1190 Old Salem Rd. NE
Albany, OR 97321
www.nicholsgardennursery.com

Territorial Seed Co.
P.O. Box 158
Cottage Grove, OR 97424
www.territorialseed.com

Victory Seed Co.
P.O. Box 192
Molalla, OR 97038
www.victoryseeds.com

D. Landreth Seed Co.
60 E. High St., Bldg. #4
New Freedom, PA 17349
www.landrethseeds.com

Heirloom Seeds
287 E. Finley Dr.
W. Finley, PA 15377
www.heirloomseeds.com

Seedway
1225 Zeager Rd.
Elizabethtown, PA 17022
www.seedway.com

W. Atlee Burpee & Co.
300 Park Ave.
Warminster, PA 18974
www.burpee.com

Seeds for the South Vegetable Seed
Warehouse
410 Whaley Pond Rd.
Granitesville, SC 29829
www.seedsforthesouth.com

High Mowing Organic Seeds
76 Quarry Rd.
Wolcott, VT 05680
www.highmowingseeds.com

The Cook's Garden
P.O. Box 535
Londonderry, VT 05148
www.cooksgarden.com

J. W. Jung Seed Co.
335 S. High St.
Randolph, WI 53957
www.jungseed.com

R. H. Shumway's
334 W. Stroud St., Ste. 1
Randolph, WI 53956
www.rhshumway.com

Vermont Bean Seed Co.
334 W. Stroud St.
Randolph, WI 53956
www.vermontbean.com

Richters Herbs
357 Hwy. 47
Goodwood, Ontario LOC 1A0
www.richters.com

Index

241